Y0-BRO-854

Tantalizing Thai Cuisine

Vinita *Atmiyanandana* Lawler

Mayhaven Publishing
P O Box 557
Mahomet, Illinois U S A

Copyright © 1993 by Vinita Atmiyanandana Lawler
First Printing 1993
Cover Design   Aaron Matthew Porter—Pella, IA
Color Separations   Oklee Graphic, Ltd—DesMoines, IA
Printing and Binding   A to Z Printing—Skokie, IL
Library of Congress Catalog Number: 93-78019
ISBN 1-878044 10-9

For My Mother

แด่แม่ที่เคารพรักยิ่ง

4

Acknowledgements

Not until after I left Thailand, to further my studies in the United States, did I realize that Thai food was one among many of the things that I had taken for granted. During the first weeks on campus, with fast food, cafeteria food, and canned food, I could not help going to bed with the quest for the real meaning of human existence on my mind. Each and every night I dreamt of various favorite dishes that my mother had cooked for me at home. In my effort to regain my peace of mind, I asked her to send me some of those recipes. Gradually, after I received and made use of them, to my surprise, school work and daily life, far away from home, was not so unbearable after all! In this manner, I practically cooked my way through college. That was because, perhaps, a little part of my quest was finally being answered. I still remember one of my good Thai friends who was full of "Joie De Vie." Whenever we gathered for a home-cooking party, she told us that she was born to eat! Maybe she was not too far off, in a way.

Thai cuisine was normally handed down from mother to daughter, especially in earlier times. I consider myself very lucky to have had this opportunity. For this reason, my heartfelt gratitude to the Guru—my mother.

For my husband, whose endless knowledge of computers and his adventurous taste for food, made any new creation possible and appreciated, I am thankful for this. I also cannot forget that my only daughter's livelihood crucially depends upon my version of Thai Gài Yang! Therefore, this dish is very important to me, too.

Well, after all has been said and done, are you now ready to try some of my recipes in this book? Bon Appetit!

Vinita Atmiyanandana Lawler
October 1992

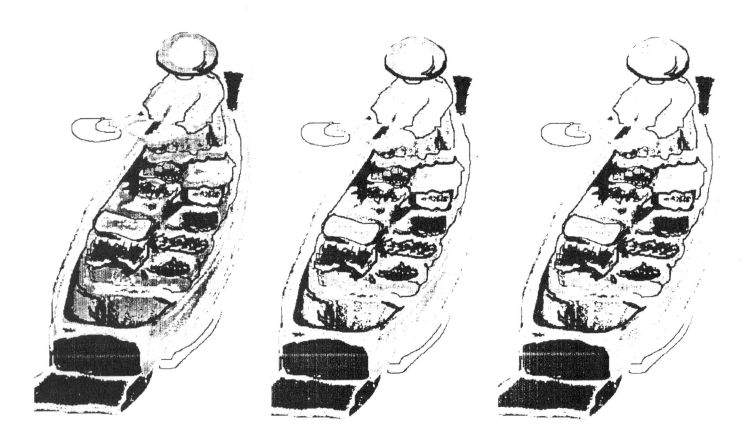

Table of Contents

Introduction

It would not take long for any visitor to notice that Thai people are poetically inclined and consider beauty a significant priority. These characteristics are reflected in all Thai art forms, including culinary art. Thai cuisine is created with three purposes in mind: a pleasing and beautiful arrangement for the eyes, meaningful and descriptive names for the ears, and tantalizing taste for the palette.

For every Thai ceremony and rite, the foods, flowers, fruits, and vegetables that are chosen have meaningful names to suit the occasion. For example, Mèe Grawp and some other noodle dishes are served at wedding parties, not just because of the taste, but also because noodles imply longevity—ideal for love and marriage!

The T'ai people were originally situated in Southern China about 7000 years ago. They moved down to form Thailand in the Golden Peninsula around 5000 years later. Miraculously, Thailand is the only country in Southeast Asia that escaped Western colonization, and perhaps, for this reason, Bangkok is the most Oriental of all the cities in the Far East. Although the influences of Chinese and Indian cuisines can be traced in some Thai dishes, Thai cuisine has its own characteristic quality. The graceful combination of salty, sour, sweet, and hot tastes is uniquely Thai.

Thai seasonings, such as fresh kaffir lime (makrut) leaves, fresh basil, coriander, lemon grass, galanga (laos or kha), rhizome (krachai), and mint, are aromatic. Thai staples include nampla (fish sauce), dried shrimp paste (kapi), turmeric, chili powder, cumin, cardamom, cinnamon, coconut, tamarind, ginger, rice, noodles, and bean threads (woon sên) etc.

Thais do not normally have knives on the dinner table, as everything is cut up in bite-sized pieces. Modern Thais eat with a fork and spoon, never chopsticks (except with noodle dishes to imitate the Chinese style). Thai restaurants in America that put chopsticks on the table follow the stereotype that all Asians eat with chopsticks. All the dishes are served at the same time, with soup in a small

Introduction

bowl on the side and rice on each individual's plate. Every diner uses a serving spoon, choosing one bite at a time from each dish and using rice as a background (to tone down the strong taste of the food). For this reason, the portion size of each dish depends on the number of dishes on the table, plus a bowl of rice, for each diner.

Every region of Thailand has its own characteristic foods and tastes. Central Thais prefer saltier and sweeter food than the people from the North, and they use more coconut milk, but less turmeric, than the Southerners. Since central Thailand is located on lower land, full of waterways and canals, the region has abundant fresh-water fish and seafood dishes to offer. On the other hand, the Southern style of food reflects a Moslem influence. Malaysian, Indonesian and Indian food use curry with spices (such as galanga, cumin, cardamom, nutmeg, turmeric). The Southern Thai style of curry, therefore, has a much stronger taste (very hot and saltier) than the curries of other regions. Southerners also use lots of coconut—which they also export—and black pepper, but less onion and less rhizome. They prefer salt to fish sauce (nampla) and also use more shrimp paste than in the northern Thailand.

Northern Thai food has a milder taste and tends to be on the sour side. The cooler climate and the Burmese influence must have something to do with this. They use plenty of vegetables, like sour egg plant, tamarind (leaves and pods), olives, and bitter melon. The northeastern region (Isan), with its dry and sandy soil, is the least fertile part of the country. Isan is extremely hot in summer and rather cool (for Thai people!) in the winter. Vegetables used in this region are papaya, bamboo shoots, cucumber, and pumpkin. The people of Isan prefer food that tastes very hot, salty and sour, all in one. They use lots of lime, tamarind, onion and, naturally—hot chili! The majority of people are farmers and have gardens of their own. They prefer tamarind to coconut milk for making curry, and use coconut milk sparingly. The people of this region use sticky rice instead of any other kind of rice.

Appetizers and Salads

Ma Haw
(Galloping Horse)

At the first bite of this appetizer, you may feel like you are on the back of your favorite horse, galloping through Le Bois de Boulogne in autumn, among red, yellow, and brown trees, with a refreshing and spicy aroma in the wind that blows in your face. That's just how I feel.

You can call this dish anything you like since each individual has his own impression. A good friend of mine cannot call it anything else but "Grasshopper." How about you?

1 fresh pineapple
1/2 lb. ground pork
1-2 medium onions (minced)
2 tablespoons dried shrimp powder
1/2 cup ground roasted peanuts (unsalted)
1 tablespoon garlic (minced)
1/2 teaspoon fresh cilantro (cut up finely)
1/2 teaspoon ground pepper

Brown sugar (to taste)
Nampla (to taste)

Cook ground pork (no oil necessary), in a pan with garlic, pepper, cilantro, and onions until well done.

Mix in dried shrimp powder, peanuts, sugar, and nampla. Then roll in all ingredients and set aside.

Cut up pineapple into 1/4 inches pieces. Arrange on a serving plate, and top with the cooked, spicy meat.

Serve in bit size pieces.

Serve 4-6.

Yum Neu Yang
(Barbeque Beef Salad)

This dish is a meal of its own. It is a typical meat salad dish of the central region, one of the most popular and favorite Thai dishes among all of my Western friends.

2 cups of beef steak, medium or rare (cut up)
1 cup cucumber (thinly sliced)
1 white onion (sliced)
1 head of romaine lettuce (washed and arranged on a serving plate)
1/2 cup of tomatoes (sliced)
2-3 red and green fresh (hot) peppers
2 cloves of garlic (minced)
1 tablespoon lime juice (or vinegar)
2 teaspoons sugar
2-3 coriander leaves
2 teaspoons nampla

Mix garlic, peppers (minced) with nampla, sugar and lime juice.

Fold in beef and the rest of the vegetables.

Sprinkle coriander leaves on top.

You can also arrange all of the vegetables on the plate, place the beef on top, then pour the sauce on when ready to serve.

Serves 4.

Laab
(Spicy Meat Salad)

This is a very popular dish that originated in the northeastern region of Thailand. It is normally very hot and spicy. You can always tone it down with less hot pepper and cool your tongue with refreshing iceberg lettuce.

5 tablespoons raw glutinous or long grain rice
1 1/2 lbs. flank steak, chicken, or pork (ground)
10 spring onions (thinly chopped)
1/2 cup lime juice
5 tablespoons nampla (fish sauce)
12 sprigs of fresh mint (minced)
1/4 tablespoon dried red-hot pepper or cayenne (ground)
2 tablespoons purple onion (minced)
1 head iceberg lettuce
10 sweet beans or asparagus (cut into 2" x 2" pieces)
1 red sweet pepper (julienne)
Dash of sugar

Heat a skillet until very hot. Add 5 tablespoons of raw rice and cook, stirring and shaking the pan until the rice is golden—about three minutes. In a blender, or food processor with a steel blade, blend the rice to a coarse powder.

Heat a wok or a deep skillet over high heat until it is smoking. Add the meat and stir fry for 15 seconds. It should be medium rare.

With a slotted spoon, transfer the meat to a bowl. Add lime juice, nampla, red pepper, and a dash of sugar. Mix well. Then spoon the mixture into a smaller bowl, Add rice powder, onion, and spring onions.

In a large platter, arrange 24 romaine lettuce leaves and asparagus—or green sweet beans—around the edge. Place the bowl of laab in the middle. Garnish with red sweet pepper and mint.

Serves 6-8.

Yum Woon Sên
(Transparent Noodle Salad)

The combination of lime juice, nampla, and sugar makes this dish deliciously refreshing. Try it and see if you agree with me. If you omit meat or shrimp, you will have a healthy vegetarian soybean-noodle salad.

5 oz. transparent noodles (dipped quickly in hot water 1-2 minutes and drained with cold water)
1/4 cup of onion (cut up)
1 tablespoon garlic (minced)
1 1/2 tablespoons fried dried shrimp—optional
12-16 boiled shrimp (deveined and cut in half)
1 cup boiled pork (ground)
1 cup boiled squid—optional
3-4 tablespoons lime juice
4 tablespoons nampla (fish sauce)
3 tablespoons brown sugar
5-6 fresh chili peppers (julienne)
2-3 tablespoons celery (cut up)
4-5 stalks of coriander leaves

Leaves of lettuce to taste
Vegetable oil (to fry garlic)

Mix sugar, nampla, and lime juice and set aside.

In a pan, heat oil (about 1 tablespoon) and fry garlic until light brown. Turn off the heat. Roll the drained noodle in the pan to coat in the garlic oil. Separate the noodles well.

On a serving plate, arrange the lettuce. Then top with noodles. Arrange the cooked pork, shrimp and squid on the noodles. Top with fried dried shrimps, pepper, onion, and celery. Decorate with the coriander leaves and pour the nampla mixture on last.

Serve at room temperature.

Serves 6-8.

Nam Prík Ong
(Thai Chili)

This is a typical and very popular side dish or condiment from northern Thailand.

1 1/2 cups lean pork or beef (ground)
1 tablespoon dried chili peppers (ground)
2 tablespoons dried shrimp powder—optional
1 tomato (cut up into tiny pieces)
1/2 medium purple onion (sliced)
3-4 cloves minced garlic
1 tablespoon minced lemon grass—optional
1 teaspoon salt
1-2 tablespoons brown sugar—optional
1-2 tablespoons lime or tamarind juice (to taste)
2 tablespoons nampla (fish sauce)
1 teaspoon shrimp paste—optional
Vegetable oil to fry
Vegetables of choice (cucumber, beans, eggplant or cabbage)

Blend lemon grass, salt, onion, garlic, chili, and shrimp paste (if used)

Heat pan with 2 tablespoons of vegetable oil to fry the mixture well, then add pork or beef.

When the meat is done, add tomato, nampla, tamarind (or lime) juice, and sugar. Adjust to taste and top with shrimp powder.

Serve with green beans, cucumber, eggplant, cabbage etc.

Serves 8.

Yum Sôm Oh
(Grapefruit Salad)

Sôm oh is a special kind of pomelo (a tropical fruit similar to large grapefruit) that has a sweeter taste than grapefruit. The province that grows sôm oh is near Bangkok, so this is a dish of central Thailand.

1 1/2 cups of grapefruit (or pomelo, if available)
1/10 lbs. of fresh shrimp or pork (cut up)
1 cup lime juice
1/2 cup brown sugar
1/2 cup nampla (fish sauce)
5 dried red peppers (fried)
1/2 cup of garlic (minced and sautéed in oil)
1/2 cup of purple onion (minced and sautéed in oil)
1/2 cup ground roasted peanuts
1/4 cup dried shrimp powder
Coriander leaves to garnish—optional

Peel and shred the grapefruit (or pomelo) and arrange on a serving plate. Peel and devein shrimp and cut in two. Boil shrimp and pork (if used).

Mix nampla, lime juice, and sugar. Pour the mixture on the shrimp and pork, then fold in the grapefruit (or pomelo).

Top the salad with dried shrimp powder, garlic and onion oil, red pepper and peanuts.

Garnish with coriander leaves, arrange lettuce leaves around the salad.

Serve cold.

Serves 6-8.

Kanom Pung Na Mòo
(Pork Toast)

This all-purpose and popular Thai appetizer is very fast and easy to make. It is suitable not only for breakfast, but also for a quick and satisfying lunch. It can be a perfect afternoon snack with tea or coffee, in which case the cucumber sauce* can be omitted.

10 pieces of bread (thinly sliced)
1 1/2 cups lean ground pork or shrimp
5 peppercorns (freshly ground)
2 coriander roots and leaves (coarsely chopped) or 1 teaspoon ground coriander
1 clove garlic (thinly sliced)
1 teaspoon salt
1-2 teaspoons Maggi sauce
2 green onions (chopped)
1 egg (well beaten)
Dash of sugar

Trim crusts off the bread and cut into quarters.

Blend pepper, coriander, garlic, and salt, then add green onions and egg to the paste.

In a bowl, mix in ground pork and stir until thoroughly blended. Add a dash of sugar and Maggi sauce to the mixture.

Spread the paste evenly on all the pieces of bread and decorate with coriander leaves.

Bake coated bread in 300°F. oven around 20-25 minutes or until golden brown.

Serves 14-16.

*For Cucumber Sauce, see Saté Thai recipe.

Nam Sod
(Refreshing Pork Snack)

Nam is a typical and well-known dish of the northern region of Thailand. The sour taste of the lime juice, when mixed with peanuts, is unique and tantalizing indeed! This dish is good with Kâo Taud.

3 cups lean ground pork
7 tablespoons lime juice
1-2 teaspoons salt
3/4 tablespoon ginger (minced)
1/2 cup thinly sliced onion
1 cup roasted peanuts
10 red and green hot peppers (to taste)
1 head lettuce or cabbage
10 stalks spring onions
10-12 stalks coriander leaves
Dash of nampla to taste

Mix the pork with 7 tablespoons lime juice and 1 teaspoon salt and squeeze off juice (use cheese cloth) into a pot.

Boil the pork juice down to 1 tablespoon, then add pork to the juice, and stir until pork is cooked.

Remove and toss, add minced ginger and onions, mix well. Adjust to taste with lime juice and nampla.

On a serving plate, arrange lettuce leaves, top the lettuce with the cooked pork, then top with peanuts, and serve with red-hot peppers, spring onions, and coriander leaves.

If you like it hot, you may also add ground red chilies.

Serves 10-12.

Yum Mamuong Kung Hang
(Spicy Mango Salad)

This is a tasty salad from central Thailand. It best represents all four tastes that belong to Thai cuisine. The fruits used for this dish have to be rather sour.

Do not mix until you are ready to serve.

1-1/2 cups green mango or tart green apple (peeled and slivered)
1/2 cup dried shrimp (fried to golden brown)
8 oz. lean pork—optional (boiled and shredded)
1/4 cup purple onion (sliced thinly)
2 tablespoons peanut brittle or dried roasted peanuts (crushed)
1 tablespoon white sesame seeds (roasted)
2 tablespoons nampla (fish sauce)
2-3 tablespoons brown sugar
5-10 red-hot peppers—optional (julienne)
4-5 cloves garlic (sliced thinly)
Vegetable oil for frying.

Mix sugar, nampla, peanuts, sesame seeds and peppers.

Heat oil and fry onion and garlic separately.

Drain oil, and set aside.

In a serving bowl, arrange mango in the middle, top with dried shrimp, pork shredded, onion and garlic.

Pour the dressing over the salad.

Serves 8.

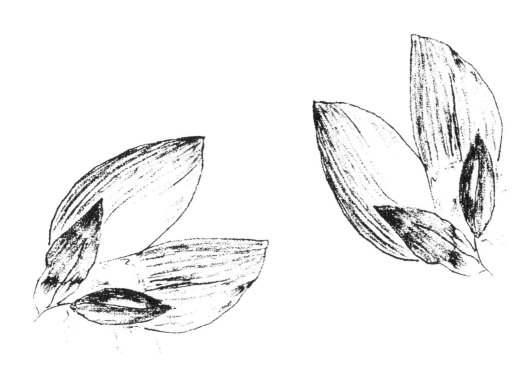

Saté Thai
(Thai Style Saté)

Like Indonesia and Malaysia, Thailand has her own version of saté. You might notice that the peanut sauce and cucumber sauce are unmistakably Thai.

2 1/2 lbs. pork chop (thin sliced)
2 tablespoons dark soy sauce
3-4 teaspoons salt
1/4-1/2 teaspoon turmeric
2 tablespoons curry powder
1-2 cups medium thick coconut milk
20-24 skewers (soaked in cold water)

Ingredients for hot peanut sauce:
3-4 tablespoons brown sugar
1 cup ground roasted peanuts
3 tablespoons nampla (fish sauce)
2 teaspoons coriander seeds (roasted)
4-5 small onions (roasted)
2-3 cloves garlic (roasted)

2 tablespoons vegetable oil
2 teaspoons cumin or fennel seeds
5 (or less) dried red peppers (soaked in water to soften)
1 teaspoon black pepper
1/4 cup tamarind liquid
1 cup thick coconut milk
1 cup thin coconut milk
1/2 teaspoon salt
3 tablespoons lemon grass (minced)
1/2 teaspoon galanga—optional (roasted)
1/2 teaspoon shrimp paste—optional

Ingredients for cucumber sauce:
1/2 cup rice wine or apple cider vinegar
2 teaspoons salt
3-4 tablespoons sugar
4-5 red, green or yellow hot peppers (slivered)
4-5 small purple onions (sliced thinly)
3-4 small cucumbers (thinly cut up)

Saté Thai cont...
(Thai Style Saté)

Wash and cut pork into 2" x 4" pieces and marinate in a mixture of dark soy sauce, salt, and curry powder for about 30 minutes.

Thread pork pieces on skewers—one on each.

Mix 1 cup of thick coconut milk with 1/4 teaspoon of turmeric and set aside. Grill or broil the pork pieces on medium heat and keep marinating both sides with the mixture of coconut and turmeric until well done.

Serve with hot peanut sauce and cucumber sauce.

To make hot peanut sauce: Blend dried red peppers, salt, shrimp paste, black pepper, roasted coriander seeds, cumin or fennel seeds, lemon grass, roasted garlic and roasted onions and galanga into a smooth paste.

In pan, fry the paste with vegetable oil and thick coconut milk until oil breaks. Adjust taste with nampla, sugar, and tamarind liquid. Add thin coconut milk to the paste and mix in ground roasted peanuts. Stir to mix well.

The hot peanut sauce should be on the thick side.

To make cucumber sauce: Boil vinegar, salt, and sugar and let cool. In a serving bowl, arrange cucumber. Top with onion and hot pepper slivers. Pour the vinegar mixture over the vegetables just before serving.

Serves 8-10.

Mòo Ping
(Skewered Marinated Pork)

Mòo Ping is an Isan version of pork saté. It is for the one who prefers a less complicated saté, but with a spicy sauce. It is a meal in itself. You can also serve Mòo Ping with bread or sticky rice.

1 1/2 lbs. lean pork (sliced into 1 1/2" x 3/4" x 2" pieces)
3/4 teaspoon white pepper
3 cloves garlic (minced)
2 teaspoons coriander seeds or 8 roots
4-5 tablespoons nampla (fish sauce)
1-2 tablespoons light soy sauce
3/4 cup coconut cream (thick)
1-2 tablespoons sugar
1/2 cup vegetable oil—optional
16-20 skewers

Ingredients for sauce:
1 tablespoon nampla
2 tablespoons lime juice
2 tablespoons light soy sauce
1 tablespoon sugar
8 stalks coriander leaves
chili powder (to taste)

Blend all the ingredients well and marinate pork pieces for about 30 minutes. Make sure every piece is well covered.

Make the sauce by mixing nampla, lime juice, soy sauce, sugar, chili powder (or fresh hot peppers), and 1 tablespoon coarsely chopped coriander leaves. Set the sauce aside.

Thread the pork pieces on skewers. Grill or broil on high heat for few minutes on both sides. Serve with lettuce and sauce.

Serves 8-10.

Popiah Thai
(Thai Egg Roll)

1/2 cup ground chicken, shrimp, or pork (thinly sliced)

25 egg roll wrappers

4 cups vegetable oil

2 mushrooms (minced)

3/4 cup bean sprouts

1/4 cup sweet basil, mint and a head of lettuce

1/2 cup transparent noodle (soak—cut into 2" - 4" pieces)

1/2 cup cabbage (thinly sliced)

1/4 cup onion and coriander leaves (minced)

1 tablespoon nampla or light soy sauce

2 teaspoons sugar

1 tablespoon garlic (minced)

1 teaspoon ground pepper

Ingredients for sauce:

1/4 cup sugar

2 tablespoons vinegar

1 teaspoon salt

3 red chili peppers

5 small cloves garlic

1/4 cup water

Fry garlic until golden brown. Add meat and mix well. Add cabbage, mushrooms and transparent noodle pieces. Adjust to taste with nampla and sugar. Continue to stir and add bean sprouts last. Remove from heat. Add a dash of pepper. Mix in onion and coriander. Stir well and let cool.

Spoon about 1-2 tablespoons of the cooked ingredients into the middle of the wrapper. Wrap well. Fry on medium heat to light brown.

To make sauce: Blend chili peppers and garlic until smooth. Mix in sugar, vinegar, salt, and water. Boil the mixture and let cool.

To serve: Arrange egg rolls in a serving plate, surrounded by basil, mint and lettuce. Serve with sauce. Serves 12-16.

Gluey Son Ruup
(Disguised Bananas)

Substitute banana in "An apple a day keeps the doctor away" and it will have the same meaning for Thai people, and probably for most Southeast Asians as well! Since there are many kinds of bananas in Thailand, and since they are very inexpensive, we eat bananas almost every day and in every form—cooked, boiled, baked, fried, steamed—even "ordained." To avoid, "What? Bananas again?" a tricky cook came up with an original idea and created this dish. See if you can detect the disguised banana here.

8 bananas
5 cups ground pork and shrimp
4 tablespoons minced garlic, black pepper, and coriander roots (save the leaves to garnish)
2 eggs
2 tablespoons nampla (fish sauce)
2 onions (minced)
2 cups of flour
2-3 tablespoons vegetable oil for frying

Dash of brown sugar
Fresh vegetables of choice
Steam bananas. Let cool and mash.

Mix mashed banana, flour, and eggs. In food processor, knead the mixture until it forms a dough. In a frying pan, heat oil and fry pork and shrimp with onion, garlic, pepper, and coriander roots until fragrant. Add nampla and a dash of sugar. Mix well and set aside.

Spread banana dough into thin sheets and cut into 3" x 3" pieces, spoon the cooked meat to put in the middle of each sheet. Wrap the banana sheet around the meat and form a small ball. Arrange all the banana balls in a steamer and use medium heat to steam the banana balls for about 10-15 minutes. Remove from heat, garnish each ball with coriander leaves. Serve with sweet soy sauce and fresh vegetables (cucumber, eggplant, pineapple, lettuce and coriander leaves). Serves 8-10.

Höy Mang Pôo Tod
(Fried Sea Mussels)

This is one of the most common, popular and healthy seafood dishes, found at almost every street-corner stand in Bangkok and its suburbs. The frying technique varies depending upon who makes it and how much time is allowed. The recipe below—restaurant style—results in a more balanced taste and a good looking dish.

15-20 smoked or fresh mussels
2 tablespoons rice flour
2 tablespoons cornstarch
1/8 tablespoon wheat flour
1/2 cup ice cold water
1/4 teaspoon salt
1 cup bean spouts
2 stalks green onions (cut into 2" x 2")
1/2 teaspoon black pepper
2 red peppers (slivered)
1 teaspoon vinegar
1 teaspoon nampla (fish sauce)
1/2-1 tablespoon vegetable oil
10 coriander leaves
dash of sugar (or to taste)

Mix rice flour, wheat flour, and cornstarch into ice cold water and salt. Dip each mussel in the flour mixture and deep fry in hot oil for three minutes.

When mussels are crispy brown, drain the oil and set aside. On high heat, stir-fry bean sprouts, red pepper, and onions with vinegar, nampla, and dash of sugar, for a few seconds.

Remove quickly into a serving plate. Spoon crispy mussels on top of the bean sprouts. Top with coriander leaves and black pepper.

Serve with Sriracha sauce.

Serves 2-4.

Saku Sâi Mòo
(Stuffed Tapioca Pearl)

This heavy snack is for afternoon tea or coffee. It is very popular in Thailand, especially in Bangkok. You can find it in almost every Thai restaurant and street-corner food stall.

1 lb. lean ground pork
5-6 cloves garlic (minced)
3 tablespoons coriander roots and leaves (minced)
1-1 1/2 teaspoons black peppers (coarsely grated)
1 teaspoon salty preserved radish—optional
1/3 cup coarsely ground peanuts
1 1/2-2 tablespoons nampla (fish sauce)
1 1/2-2 tablespoons brown sugar
1/3 cup minced purple onion or 1-2 small onions
2 lbs. tapioca pearls
Vegetables: Romaine lettuce, coriander leaves, and red peppers (minced in tiny pieces)
Wax paper (cut into 2" x 2" pieces)
1/2 cup oil to fry garlic

Divide half of the garlic and fry in hot oil until light brown. Spoon the garlic with oil from the pan and set aside.

Blend the rest of the garlic with coriander roots and leaves and black pepper. Stir fry garlic mixture in the same pan (do not wash the garlic off), with pork, salty radish, peanuts, nampla, sugar and minced onion. Mix well—until it almost dries up. Remove from heat and set aside.

Knead tapioca pearls in very warm water, form into small balls. Flatten each ball and spoon the cooked pork into the middle of each ball. Fold in the tapioca to cover the pork. Lay them about 1" apart on a piece of wax paper and steam until all the tapioca becomes transparent (about 15-25 minutes).

Remove from heat. Arrange them in a serving plate and garnish each ball with fried garlic oil. Serve with vegetables and fresh hot pepper pieces. Serves 6.

Naatang
(Uplifting Dip)

This is very uplifting for your taste buds. One tip—to fry the sizzling rice sheets or chips, to perfection, the oil should be so hot that when you drop a chip in, it pops up right away. Then turn the chip over and spoon it out immediately. To leave it a second longer will result in a yellowish or burned chip. Once in a while, lower the heat a bit so the oil does not become too hot.

2 cups ground lean pork

1 cup ground shrimp or dried shrimp powder

1/2 cup roasted peanuts (coarsely ground)

3 cups medium thin coconut milk

1/2-3/4 cup onion (minced)

3 tablespoons nampla (fish sauce)

2-3 tablespoons brown sugar

2 tablespoons tamarind liquid

2 1/2 tablespoons garlic (minced)

2 teaspoons coriander roots— 6-7 stalks (minced)

1 teaspoon ground pepper

2 1/2 cups vegetable oil

12-16 pieces (2" x 2") sizzling rice sheets, shrimp chips, or any other kind you prefer.

1-2 hot chili peppers (slivered)

Blend the garlic, pepper, and coriander roots into a paste. Separate the leaves and set aside for garnishing. Boil 2 1/4 cups of coconut milk and add the paste. Mix well. Mix the pork and shrimp into the rest of the coconut milk and add to the pot. Stir the mixture very well and cook on low heat. Add nampla, sugar, tamarind liquid, onion, and peanuts. Keep stirring. The mixture should be smooth. Adjust the thickness of the sauce to your liking with coconut milk. Heat to boiling. Remove immediately from the heat. Garnish with coriander leaves and red peppers.

To serve: arrange the rice sheets in a serving plate with the bowl of sauce in the middle. You could also serve Naatung with shrimp chips, fish chips, rice chips, or fried wonton sheets. Serves 14-16.

Mieng Mae Poow
(Mother-in-Law Appetizer)

Why this name? It's not for me to say. The interpretation should be left to your own imagination since you are going to be the one to create the dish!

2 1/2 cups shredded coconut flakes (roasted)
1/2 cup dried shrimp powder
1/2 cup roasted peanuts (unsalted)
2-3 tablespoons fresh ginger (minced)
1/4 cup purple onion (minced and roasted)
2 tablespoons nampla (fish sauce)
1/4 cup thick tamarind liquid or lime juice
1/2 cup brown sugar
red-hot peppers (to taste)
Use sour tasting fruits: green mango, green apple, grapefruit or pomelo etc. (peel and slice into bite-sizes)
Use green vegetables: lettuce, cabbage, or collard green etc. (wash and cut into 4" x 4" pieces)
8-10 fresh red or yellow hot chili peppers (minced)

Boil nampla, sugar, tamarind liquid (or lime juice), and hot pepper to taste. Mix in coconut and shrimp powder and spoon into a small bowl.

On a snack tray: set the small sauce bowl in the middle and arrange peanuts, ginger, and onions—each separately—around it. Then arrange fruit pieces around them and vegetables next to the fruits.

To serve: drop fruit pieces on a vegetable sheet topped with ginger, peanuts and onion. Then, spoon the sauce to top them and wrap the leave to form a mouthful.

Serves 4-6.

Yum Polamai
(Tropical Fruit Salad)

Yum Polamai is a colorful and tasty dish from the central region. It is a good example of what I mean by Thai culinary art.

1/2 cup vegetable oil

1/4 cup sugar

5 tablespoons lime juice

1 teaspoon salt

1/4 teaspoon mustard

1/3 cup thinly sliced shallots

1 teaspoon dried shrimp powder

1/4 teaspoon ground red pepper

1/4 cup coarsely ground peanuts

1/2 cup of banana (sliced)

1/2 cup green mango (sliced)

1/2 cup watermelon (cut up)

1/2 cup pineapple (diced)

1/2 cup orange or you can also use pears, grapes, or grapefruit (minced)

Combine all the fruits and arrange them in a serving bowl and set aside.

Mix oil, sugar, lime juice, salt, mustard, and shallots. Pour the mixture over the fruits and top with dried shrimp powder, ground red pepper, and peanuts.

Serves 12.

Yum Tang Kwa
(Cucumber Salad)

This dish was created to make full use of the cucumber. Its cool and refreshing quality help tone down hot and spicy dishes and soothe your mouth.

2 green cucumbers
1 small onion
2 tablespoons dried shrimp powder
1 or 2 red peppers—optional (seeded and slivered)
1 or 2 tablespoons crushed peanuts
2 tablespoons nampla
2 tablespoons lime juice (or to taste)
2 tablespoons sugar

Peel and grate cucumber coarsely. Discard seed.

Slice onion and arrange vegetables on a serving plate with cucumber first and onion next. Sprinkle dried shrimp powder on top. Garnish with red peppers.

Mix sugar, nampla, and lime juice in a bowl. Pour the mixture over the salad just before serving.

Top with coarsely crushed peanuts. Serve slightly chilled.

Serves 6.

Sôm Tum
(Carrot and/or Papaya Salad)

This is the most typical dish of the northeastern region. It became a very popular dish all over the country. In contrast to cucumber salad (which is used to tone down hot and spicy dishes) Sôm Tum is used to enhance the flavor of milder dish—especially gài yang.

3-4 cups grated green papaya
1 cup grated carrot
1/2 cup dried shrimp powder
5-7 cloves garlic (minced)
4 dried red peppers (soaked)
1/2-1 tablespoon sugar (or to taste)
2 tablespoons nampla (or to taste)
3 big limes or, 4-5 tablespoons tamarind liquid
1/2-1 teaspoon black pepper
2-3 red-hot peppers (slivered)

Blend dried peppers with garlic, then mix in carrot and papaya, nampla, tamarind liquid, sugar, lime juice, dried shrimp powder, and black pepper.

Mix well and adjust taste.

Garnish with red peppers.

Serves 6-8.

Salad Kag
(Southern Style Salad)

Food from Southern Thailand, where the majority of the people are Muslim, shows influences from the neighboring countries of Malaysia and Indonesia. This salad is an example. Thais also prefer to add chicken or pork (boiled and shredded), but this original dish is very delicious with just tofu and fried potatoes.

2-3 dried red peppers (soaked in cold water and deseeded)
6 pearl (or very small) onions
5 whole black peppers
2 cups medium coconut milk
2-3 tablespoons ground roasted peanuts (unsalted)
1/2 cup tamarind liquid
2-3 teaspoons salt
2-3 tablespoons brown sugar
Dash of curry powder—optional
1 head of romaine lettuce (cut into 2" x 2" pieces)
1 big onion (sliced thinly)
10 pickle cucumbers (sliced)

10 Italian tomatoes (sliced)
1 1/2 cups bean sprouts (soft boiled quickly)
3 hard boiled eggs (sliced thinly)
1 cup fried white tofu (slivered)
1/2 cup fried potatoes or chips (unsalted)

Blend dried red peppers, black peppers, and pearl onions into smooth paste. Fry the paste with 2 cups of coconut milk, on low heat until oil breaks. Add ground peanuts, tamarind liquid, salt, brown sugar, and a dash of curry powder—if you like. Adjust to your taste. The dressing should be medium thick with three balancing tastes: sweet, salty and sour. The degree of hotness is up to you. Reduce or increase the red-hot peppers.

On a serving plate, arrange lettuce, cucumber, onion, tomato, boiled eggs, and bean sprouts and top with the dressing just before serving. Add fried tofu and potato chips last. Serves 6-8.

Vegetables

Pad Woon Sên
(Fried Bean Thread)

This is one of my favorite noodle dishes, probably because I like mung bean noodles (bean thread or transparent noodles) and because it is difficult to cook exactly the way it should be. The noodles should be soaked in cold water to maintain crispiness. When folding in to stir fry with other ingredients, you have to work very fast and try to coat the noodles in the sauce evenly.

1 cup bean thread (soaked in cold water to soften and drained)
2 teaspoons spring onion (minced)
1 teaspoon fresh ginger (minced)
1-2 tablespoons ground roasted peanuts—unsalted
1-2 stalks of celery (cut into 1" x 1" pieces)
1 cup bean sprouts (cleaned)
1-2 eggs—optional
1 tablespoon nampla (fish sauce)
1 teaspoon sugar
2 tablespoons thin soy or Kikkoman soy sauce

3-4 tablespoons vegetable oil
1 1/2 cup of Napa or Chinese lettuce (cut thinly)
1 cup hed hunu, wood fungus, or cloud-ear fungus (soaked in warm water for 15 minutes)—optional
Dash of Sriracha or tabasco sauce—optional
2-3 teaspoons water or stock (to taste)
2-3 stalks coriander leaves
Dash of black pepper

In large pan or wok, heat oil and scramble the egg quickly with green onion and ginger. Then add bean thread with water or stock.

Stir fry quickly and thoroughly. Mix in bean sprouts, celery, nampla, soy sauce, sugar, lettuce, wood fungus (if used), and a dash of Sriracha.

Remove from heat and top with peanut and coriander leaves and a dash of black pepper. Serve hot. Serves 4-6.

Pad Tou Ngórg Hou Pag Gaad
(Fried Bean Sprouts & Parsnips)

If you like bean sprouts, you will like this dish. It is very nutritious. With a good portion of hot rice, you will have a full meal.

1 1/2 cups parsnips (slivered into 2" x 2" pieces)
1 1/2 cups bean sprouts (cleaned)
1-2 teaspoons garlic (minced)
1/2 cup yellow tofu (slivered into 2" x 2" pieces)
1 tablespoon each oyster sauce and Maggi sauce
1 teaspoon sugar
Vegetable oil to fry
Dash of black pepper
Heat oil and fry garlic with tofu and parsnips for a few seconds.

Turn heat on high. Add sugar and both sauces, then bean sprouts, and stir fry quickly.

Remove from heat while vegetables are still fresh and crispy. Sprinkle with black pepper.

Serve hot with rice.

Serves 8-10.

Kâo Pad Mamuong
(Mango Fried Rice)

Another version of Thai fried rice (see Kâo Pad Thai Tae). Mamuong will give you a special sour taste to the dish. You could use green apple as a substitute if you can not get hold of any mango.

1 green mango (cut into bite-sizes)
2 cups onions (cut up)
2 cups green beans (cut into 2" x 2" pieces)
8 cups cooked rice
2 cups sliced mushrooms
2 cups cut-up tomatoes
1/2 cup fresh ginger (minced)
1 tablespoon brown sugar (or to taste)
1-2 tablespoons thin soy sauce
1-2 tablespoons garlic (minced)
Dash black pepper
Vegetable oil to fry

In a wok, heat oil to fry garlic until golden.

Add mushrooms, ginger, soy sauce, sugar and black pepper.

Add mango, rice, onions, and tomatoes and stir fry well. Drop in green beans to mix well.

Remove from heat and serve hot.

Serves 10-12.

Pad Fakthong
(Fried Pumpkin & Egg)

Do not throw away your pumpkins after the Halloween season. This is one way to turn the pumpkin into a delicious dish, fast and easy, too.

1/2 lb. pumpkin (sliced thinly 2" x 2" pieces)
1 egg
2 tablespoons vegetable oil
2-3 teaspoons brown sugar
1 1/2 tablespoon nampla (fish sauce)
4 small cloves garlic (minced)
Dash of pepper

Fry garlic in oil until light gold and add pumpkin pieces.

While pumpkin is cooking, add nampla and sugar.

Make a space in the middle and break egg in and cook.

Then roll in everything to fry few more minutes.

When the pumpkin is done, remove from heat. Dash pepper on top.

Serve hot with rice and other dishes.

Serves 2-4.

Yum Saam See
(Three Color Salad)

Three is just a minimum figure. You will agree that this colorful salad is the proof that appearance adds to the taste of any dish. Create your own salad with a Thai tangy and exotic dressing. A nice compliment from your guests is in store for you!

1/2 cabbage (slice thinly)
1 big carrot (peel and grate coarsely)
1 boiled red or green bell pepper (slice thinly)
1 red pepper (deseeded)
6-7 cloves garlic (minced)
2 tablespoons sugar
2 tablespoons lime juice
1 teaspoon salt
1 teaspoon light soy sauce
1 tablespoon ground roasted peanuts
1 tablespoon sliced tofu (fried)
1 tablespoon roasted coconut flakes
1 tablespoon thinly sliced purple onion

Blend garlic, red pepper with lime juice, sugar, salt and soy.

Arrange cabbage, carrot, and bell pepper in a bowl.

Pour the mixture over and toss well.

Top with onion, peanuts, fried tofu, and coconut flakes.

Serves 4.

Mara Pad Kài
(Egg with Bitter Melon)

Who said bitter melon is too bitter to eat? Try this method and you would agree that if Vodka does not taste too bitter for you, bitter melon is just a piece of cake!

1 bitter melon (cut in half, deseeded and sliced thinly)
1-2 eggs
2 tablespoons thin soy sauce
1 1/2 teaspoons garlic (minced)
1/4 cup vegetable oil
1-2 teaspoons salt (to taste)
1 teaspoon sugar
1 teaspoon rice flour
Dash of pepper

Soak bitter melon pieces in salt water for at least 10 minutes, then rinse with warm water and dry.

Beat eggs with soy sauce, salt, sugar and rice flour and mix in the melon pieces.

In a pan, fry garlic in oil until golden brown.

Pour the egg mixture in and rotate the pan so that the melon and egg are equally cooked.

Turn over when both sides are puffy and light brown.

Remove from heat and sprinkle with pepper.

Serve hot with Sriracha sauce and rice.

Serves 2-4.

Pad Pug Preaw Wan
(Fried Varieties)

This is an all season dish and is good with just about everything on the table. It can also be served just with rice as a light lunch.

1 head of cabbage (sliced)
1 cucumber (sliced length-wise)
1 onion (cut up)
4-5 stalks green onions (cut 2" x 2")
2-3 carrots (sliced thinly)
2 radishes (or parsnips) (julienne)
3 stalks celery (julienne)
2 tablespoons soy sauce
2 tablespoons brown sugar
2 tablespoons nampla
2 tablespoons tamarind liquid (or rice vinegar)
1 tablespoon oyster sauce
2 tablespoons vegetable oil
2 cloves garlic (minced)
1 teaspoon ginger (minced)

Mix soy sauce, sugar, nampla, and tamarind liquid and set aside.

Fry garlic and ginger in oil until fragrant.

Add carrot, radish, cabbage, celery, cucumber, onion, and green onion, last.

Mix in the prepared sauce.

Sprinkle oyster sauce and stir to mix.

Do not fry more than 1-2 minutes. With this method, you will be able to keep all the vegetables crispy and fresh.

Serve hot with rice.

Serves 8-10.

Soups

Jub Chai
(Spicy Vegetable Soup)

The phrase "jub chai" is an idiom for "anything goes." You can, therefore, apply this method to this recipe. The result will be just as tasty.

6 cups water
6 stalks coriander with roots (clean and separate leaves)
5-10 cloves garlic (crushed)
5-10 black peppers (crushed)
2-3 tablespoons vegetable oil
1/2 cup diced tofu—optional
1 cup of cabbage (cut up)
1 cup Napa lettuce (cut up)
1 cup collard greens (cut up)
1 cup parsnips (cut up)
1 cup Chinese mushrooms (cut up)
1/2 cup of diced celery (diced)
1 cup of transparent noodle
2 tablespoons sugar

3-4 tablespoons soy sauce
Dash of nampla to taste

Blend garlic, pepper, and coriander roots and stalks (cut up).

Heat oil to fry the mixture.

Drop all the vegetables in to stir fry very quickly.

Add water, tofu (if used), sugar, soy sauce, and a dash nampla..

Lower the heat until you are ready to serve, then turn up the heat and drop the noodles in for only a few seconds. serve at once.

Serves 8-10.

Gang Chud
(Meat Ball & Squid Soup)

This is a mild but tasty soup for any Thai dinner. It is handy to have around to fall back on in case the hotness or spiciness of other dishes begins to get to you.

1 cup lean ground pork
1/2 cup squid (cleaned and cut 1" x 1")
1/2 cup green onion (finely chopped)
1/2-1 teaspoon white pepper
2 teaspoons finely minced garlic
1/2-1 teaspoon salt
1 teaspoon wine (or sake)
1 teaspoon garlic oil (minced garlic fried in oil)
1 teaspoon coriander seed
2-3 stalks of coriander leaves (cut-up)
2-3 tablespoons nampla (fish sauce)
6-7 leaves of Napa lettuce or cabbage (cut into 2" x 2" pieces)
1 zucchini or cucumber (cut into cubes)
1 cup of mushrooms—hed hunu or wood fungus (soaked in water and cut in half)
8-9 cups of chicken stock (or water)
Dash of sugar and dash of pepper

Mix ground pork with the finely minced garlic, coriander seeds, pepper, green onion, salt, wine, and one tablespoon of nampla. Stuff the pork mixture in the middle of the squid pieces.

In a pot, bring the soup stock to a boil. Drop the stuffed squids into the soup one at a time. Continue to boil on medium heat for about 5-7 minutes.

Add vegetables to the soup—mushrooms last. Bring to boil again, then adjust the taste with nampla, dash of sugar, and black pepper.

Before serving, top with garlic oil, coriander leaves, and a dash of pepper. Serve hot. Serves 8-10.

Gang Liang
(Southern Vegetable Soup)

Old folks advised women who had just delivered their babies to consume this healthy soup as much as possible, especially if they intended to breast feed their babies.

4-5 cups water
3/4 teaspoon shrimp paste (or anchovy paste)
1 teaspoon salt
1 teaspoon black pepper
6 pearl onions
3/4 teaspoon ground rhizome or 5 dried pieces
1/2 cup pumpkin (1" x 1" pieces)
1/2 cup sweet potato (1" x 1" pieces)
4-5 ears young corn—optional
1 cup cucumber (1" x 1" pieces)
1 cup squash or zucchini
1/2 cup dried shrimp (soaked to soften)
1 cup spinach
1/2 cup sweet basil

Boil 4-6 cups water.

Blend shrimp paste, salt, black pepper, and onions. Spoon into the boiling water. Then, add rhizome, pumpkin, potato, corn, cucumber, squash or zucchini, dried shrimps, spinach, and basil last.

Serve hot.

Serves 8-10.

Tom Sôm Chaow Ngór
(Rambutan Soup)

Rambutan is a delightful tropical fruit with white juicy meat. It is one of my favorites.

2 tablespoons purple onion (minced)
2 1/2 teaspoons ground pepper
1/2 teaspoon shrimp paste
2 teaspoons salt
3-4 tablespoons brown sugar
3/4 cup tamarind liquid
2-3 tablespoons nampla (or to taste)
30 rambutans (can or fresh—without seeds)
2-3 cups ground chicken meat
1/4 cup ginger (minced)
1/2 cup green onions (cut up)
2 fresh red peppers (slivered)
6 cups water
1/4 cup coriander leaves to garnish

Blend onion, black pepper, shrimp paste, and 1 teaspoon salt until smooth. Set aside.

Make small balls of ground chicken mixed with 1 teaspoon salt. Stuff the chicken balls in the rambutans.

In a soup pot, boil water and blend in the onion mixture, then add sugar, nampla, tamarind liquid, stuffed rambutans, and any remaining chicken balls.

When the chicken balls are cooked, adjust taste and add ginger and green onion.

Top with sliced red pepper and coriander leaves before serving.

Serves 8-10.

Gang Sôm Isan
(Northeastern Garden Sour Soup)

Here is an example of the strong and very tasty soup of Isan, loaded with healthy vegetables. One bowl of this soup with steamed rice can be quite satisfying.

2 lbs. sliced flank beef
10 ears of baby corn (chopped thinly)
10 mushrooms (cut in half)
8-10 Italian tomatoes
8 sweet beans (cut into 1" pieces)
8 yellow and red chili peppers
10 fresh peppercorns (or 15 dried)
3/4 cup sweet basil
8-10 pearl onions or purple onions
1/2 teaspoon shrimp paste
6 teaspoons nampla (or to taste)
6 teaspoons lime juice (or to taste)
1-2 teaspoons ginger (minced)
1 teaspoon brown sugar
8-10 cups water

Blend chili peppers, onions, shrimp paste, and ginger.

Boil 8-10 cups water and mix in the paste.

Add beef pieces, sugar, nampla, and lime juice.

Drop in baby corn, mushrooms, sweet beans, tomatoes, and peppercorns, last. Top with basil.

Serve immediately.

Serves 12-14.

Soup Gài Kreung Ted
(Chicken Spiced Soup)

This spiced chicken soup is one of my mom's specialties. When sick with a bad cold, it always hits the spot. It can also serve as a full meal with rice. It is one of my mother-in-law's favorite Thai dishes!

2 lbs. chicken (cut into 3" x 3" pieces)
3/4 tablespoon cinnamon (3" stick)
1 nutmeg (crushed)
5-7 cardamoms (crushed)
1 1/2 teaspoons mace
5-6 cloves
4-5 potatoes (peeled and cut in 4 pieces)
4-5 onions (peeled and cut in 4 pieces)
2 tablespoons nampla (fish sauce)
2 tablespoons Worcestershire sauce
Dash of salt and pepper
Vegetable oil to fry

Fry chicken chunks until light brown on all sides.

Add a dash of salt and pepper in the pan and stir again.

Remove the chicken pieces into a soup pot and cover them with water.

Bring the soup to a boil and add nutmeg, cardamom, mace, cloves, and cinnamon.

Cover and continue to boil for 5-7 minutes more, then add potatoes.

When potatoes are cooked, add onions. When the onions are transparent, add nampla and remove from the heat.

Drop in Worcestershire sauce before serving.

Serves 4-6.

Gang Sôm Pag Tai
(Southern Style Sour Soup)

"Pag Tai" refers to southern Thailand, which favors very strong and hot cuisine. This is an example of sour soup that also has turmeric, a favorite ingredient of the region, in it.

1 1/2 lbs. shrimps (run knife through the backs to clean and leave the tails)
1/2 pineapple (cut in cubes)
6-12 dried red-hot peppers (to taste)
15-20 small garlics (crushed)
1-2 teaspoons shrimp paste
1/4 cup of rice
1/2-1 teaspoon turmeric (fresh if possible)
4 teaspoons nampla
4 teaspoons lime juice
4-5 cups of water

Blend peppers, rice, garlic, shrimp paste, and turmeric into a paste.

Boil water in a soup pot and mix in the paste.

While the mixture is boiling, drop in the pineapple cubes, shrimps, and add nampla and lime juice.

Serve hot.

Serves 4-6.

Gang Leung
(Yellow Spicy Soup)

This is another typical southern-style hot and spicy seafood soup. It is delicious when served with rice and vegetables. This soup has four strong tastes.

2 1/2 cups scallops

1/2 cup fish fillet

20 red and yellow hot peppers (Prík Kee Nùu preferred)

1/3 teaspoon salt

1 teaspoon turmeric (fresh preferred)

2-3 tablespoons garlic (minced)

2-3 tablespoons purple onions (minced)

1-2 teaspoons shrimp paste

6-7 cups water

4-5 cups pineapple chunks

5 tablespoons nampla

1-2 tablespoons sugar

9-10 tablespoons tamarind liquid

Blend peppers, salt, turmeric, garlic, onion, fish fillet, and shrimp paste. Mix water with the paste and bring to boil.

While boiling, drop in pineapple chunks, nampla, sugar, and tamarind liquid.

When the soup is boiling hard again, add the scallops.

After the scallops are done, remove from heat.

Serve hot with rice, vegetables of choice, and other dishes.

Serves 8-10.

Poultry

Gài Yang
(Thai Barbeque Chicken)

As I mentioned before, this dish is very important to me because my daughter has grown up on it. I also have learned that it never fails me whenever I have a house party that involves children. It is a miracle!

If you are pressed for time, garlic powder can be substituted for fresh garlic. Coconut milk can be omitted.

1 chicken (cut into parts and skinned)
1-1 1/2 tablespoons nampla (or salt)
20 seeds of fresh black pepper (crushed)
1-2 cloves of garlic (minced)
10-15 cilantro leaves and roots (cut up and crushed)
1/4 cup sake or wine
1/4 cup coconut milk—optional
1 tablespoon thin soy sauce
1 tablespoon brown sugar

Blend all ingredients well. Marinate chicken parts abo minutes (or less).

Barbeque, broil, or bake in 350° F. oven until brown on both sides.

Serve with steamed or sticky rice (with or without sauce).

Serves 4-6.

To make the sauce for the chicken, mix 3-4 minced hot peppers (or Sriracha sauce) with nampla, minced garlic and add brown sugar to taste.

Sôm tum is an excellent side dish for Gài Yang.

Gài Grawp Preaw Wan
(Crispy Sweet Sour Chicken)

This is a perfect chicken dish for people who do not care for hot peppers.

1 cup chicken fillet (cut into 3" pieces)
3 egg whites (slightly beaten)
4 tablespoons cornstarch
1/2 cup vegetable oil to fry
1/4 cup lime juice
1 cup water
3 tablespoons honey
1 teaspoon ginger (minced)
2 tablespoons white sugar
1 1/2 teaspoons salt (or to taste)
1 tablespoon water
1-2 spring onions
4-5 sliced gingers

Mix egg whites and 2 1/2 tablespoons cornstarch to coat chicken pieces well.

Heat oil to medium and fry the chicken pieces until golden brown. Drain oil and arrange in a serving plate.

Mix 1 1/2 tablespoons of cornstarch with 1 tablespoon of water and set aside.

Leave two tablespoons of oil in the pan to fry sliced ginger. Then, mix in lime juice, water, minced ginger, honey, sugar, and salt. Stir well. When the mixture is boiling, blend in the cornstarch mixture. Keep stirring.

When the cornstarch is cooked, pour the sweet and sour mixture on top of the chicken pieces and garnish with spring onions.

Serves 8.

Keow Wan Gài
(Green Chicken Curry)

This green curry paste is also very good with beef or pork. It is a common dish of central Thailand.

2 1/2 lbs. chicken breast (cut up)
5 cups coconut milk (set aside 3 spoons of thick milk)
1/2 cup green peas
1-2 egg plants (sliced in bite sizes)
2 tablespoons nampla (fish sauce)
1 tablespoon brown sugar
1 cup basil leaves
3-5 kaffir lime leaves
10-20 fresh green hot peppers (or to taste)
1 tablespoon salt
3 stalks lemon grass (clean and mince the white parts, discarding the green leaves)
3 slices galanga
2 teaspoons coriander seeds
1 teaspoon cumin
3 tablespoons onions (cut up)
1/2 cup minced garlic
1 teaspoon shrimp paste

Separate out 3-4 of the green hot peppers and sliver them for garnishing. Blend remaining fresh hot peppers, salt, lemon grass, galanga, coriander seeds, cumin, onion, garlic, and shrimp paste into a paste. Set aside.

Boil coconut milk and add chicken pieces until cooked.

In a pan with thick coconut milk, fry the prepared curry paste with Kaffir lime leaves. Then, spoon the chicken pieces to mix in the paste, blend in the rest of the coconut milk. Add nampla, sugar.

When the curry is boiling add egg plant and green peas, cook for few minutes more and remove from heat. Garnish with fresh pepper slivers and basil leaves. Serve hot with rice or Thai rice noodles. Serves 8-10.

Gang Massaman
(Southern Style Curry)

It is obvious that Gang Massaman has been influenced by the Muslim way of cooking. If you love Indian food, you will like this curry, too. It is always a hit at parties.

2 1/2 lbs. chicken or beef or pork (cut in bite sizes and fried until golden brown)
10-12 fresh shallots
6 cups medium-thick coconut milk
1/2 lb. boiled potato (cut up)
1/4-1/2 cup nampla (or salt to taste)
1/4-1/2 cup brown sugar
3/4 cup unsalted roasted peanuts
1/4-1/2 cup tamarind liquid

Ingredients for Curry Paste:
9 dried roasted hot peppers (deseeded)
7 toasted shallots or 1/2 cup of cut-up onions
7 small toasted cloves of garlic
1 tablespoon roasted shrimp paste

12 black peppers
1 tablespoon coriander seeds (or fresh stalks with roots)
2 tablespoons toasted lemon grass (minced)
3 slices toasted galanga (about 2 teaspoons)
1 teaspoon toasted cumin
5 cardamom seeds (about 1 tablespoon minced cardamom)
5 cloves
1 cinnamon stick (about 1" long)
1/4 teaspoon nutmeg

Blend all of the curry ingredients into a paste. Boil coconut milk, then lower the heat to medium and drop meat pieces into the pot. Spoon about 5 tablespoons of coconut milk into a pan and fry the curry paste until fragrant. Mix the curry paste in with the meat. Simmer until meat is tender. While simmering, add the fresh shallots, boiled potatoes, nampla, sugar, peanuts, and tamarind liquid. Adjust to taste and serve immediately with rice or bread.

Serves 10-12.

Gang Benjarong Gài
(Five Gems Curry)

This is a creation of the central Thais. Just the appearance of this beautiful dish is worth the cooking effort—let alone the unusual taste.

3 lbs. chicken breasts
3 cups medium-thin coconut milk (4 cups thin and 1/2 cup thick)
1/3 cup nampla (fish sauce)
1/4 cup brown sugar
2 cups sweet basil leaves
10 kaffir lime leaves
1 cup green peas
1 cup Italian tomatoes
1 cup green seedless grapes
1 cup chunk pineapple
8 fresh red-hot peppers (deseeded and slivered)
10-15 dried red peppers or for milder taste, use 5-6 Mexican finger peppers
2 teaspoons galanga

2 teaspoons salt
1 1/2-2 tablespoons coriander stalks with roots (minced)
1/2 cup fresh or dried lemon grass (minced)
4-5 tablespoons chopped garlic
4-5 tablespoons chopped onion
1-1 1/2 teaspoons shrimp paste
3 teaspoons roasted ground coriander seed
2 teaspoons roasted ground cumin

Blend the last 10 ingredients until smooth. Cut up chicken breasts into small pieces. Prepare and wash vegetables and fruits. In a pan, boil the medium coconut milk and mix into paste. Stir fry until fragrant and oil is separated. Blend in thin coconut milk. While it is still boiling, drop in chicken pieces, green peas, tomatoes, grapes, pineapple chunks, kaffir leaves, and peppers. Adjust the taste with nampla and sugar, then mix in thick coconut milk and top with basil leaves before serving. You can dilute the curry with water to taste while it is boiling. Serve with rice. Serves 10-12.

Gài Yang Sòng Kreung
(Chicken From Southern Thailand)

You can see Muslim influence on this chicken dish. It is totally different from the Isan style of Gài Yang.

1 1/2 lbs. chicken breast (skinless and boneless preferred)

4 tablespoons margarine (or butter)

1/2 tablespoon coriander seed

1 teaspoon cumin

5 stalks fresh coriander (with roots)

10 black peppers

5-6 cloves garlic

1/2 cup pearl onions (or purple onions)

3/4 teaspoon turmeric

1 1/2 teaspoons salt

1-2 tablespoons Worcestershire sauce

2 tablespoons white wine

Coat chicken in margarine and set aside.

Blend all the ingredients until smooth and marinate the chicken pieces for 20-30 minutes.

Broil or bake (300° F.) them until light brown on both sides.

Serve with rice and hot sauce (if preferred).

Serves 4-6.

Gang Tom Jeiw
(Sour Chicken Curry)

Originally this curry was made with beef. Later chicken was used more. This curry is perfect for people who want to limit fats, especially those in coconut milk.

2 lbs. chicken pieces (breasts and thighs)
5-6 cups water
10 black peppers
2-3 stalks coriander (separate leaves and roots)
10 cloves garlic (crushed)
7-8 slices of galanga
7 pearl onions
3 stalks of lemon grass (cut into 1" pieces)
10-15 chili peppers (or to taste)
4 tablespoons nampla (fish sauce)
3 tablespoons brown sugar
Juice of 1 lime
2 tablespoons tamarind liquid

Blend black peppers, coriander roots, garlic, and galanga.

Boil six cups of water.

Drop in chicken pieces, then onions, lemon grass, and chili peppers.

When chicken is tender, adjust by balancing three tastes (to your liking) with nampla, sugar, tamarind liquid, and lime juice.

Top with coriander leaves. Serve with rice.

Serves 6-8.

59

Preawan Saam Yang
(Sweet & Sour Trio)

I created this dish for a cooking demonstration on a television program. The studio crew and members of the audience had such a feast that I, did not have more than one bite—a bittersweet memory indeed!

4 chicken breasts
4 pork chops
1 lb. shrimp (peeled and deveined)
1/2 cup of cut up pineapple
1/2 cup of cut up cucumber (partly peeled)
1/2 cup of cut up tomato
1/2 cup white onion
1-2 bell green and red peppers (sliced)
1 bunch of green onions (cut into 2" long pieces)
2-3 carrots (cut up)
1 teaspoon of garlic (minced)
2-3 tablespoons vegetable oil
1 tablespoon catchup
1 tablespoon nampla (fish sauce)
2 tablespoons soy sauce
1/2 cup of vinegar
2-3 tablespoons of brown sugar
1/2-1 tablespoon cornstarch
1-1 1/2 cups of white wine or sake
dash of salt and red and black pepper to taste

Cut chicken and pork into small cubes and marinate with shrimp, in wine, garlic, one tablespoon soy sauce, salt and pepper for at least 15 minutes. Mix vinegar, rest of soy sauce, sugar, cornstarch, and nampla. Set aside. Heat vegetable oil in frying pan. Fry marinated meats until light brown (shrimp last). Spoon them up, drain, and arrange on serving plate. Add carrot, white onion, and bell pepper to stir fry quickly. Pour out excess oil from pan. Blend in catchup and sauce (mixed above). Add green onions, tomato, pineapple, and cucumber to the sauce. Adjust taste with salt and red or black pepper. Top the meats and shrimp with the sweet and sour sauce and serve with rice. Serves 12.

Gài Pad Horapa
(Chicken Breast With Basil)

Horapa refers to basil in Thai. Any variety of basil you like will do the trick. This dish is perfect for lunch, especially when you add rice to stir fry with it. Gài Pad Horapa is available almost in every Thai restaurant in Bangkok. This dish is not only delicious, but also very easy to make. It will take you not more than 10-15 minutes.

2 1/2 lbs. skinless chicken breast (cut up in bite-sizes)
3 teaspoons minced garlic
1 1/2 cups purple onion (sliced into 1/4" pieces)
4 tablespoons vegetable oil
3 tablespoons nampla (or to taste)
1 1/2 tablespoons brown sugar
1 1/2 tablespoons vinegar
6 red, green, or yellow hot peppers (julienne)
1 1/2 cups sweet basil leaves
Fry garlic in medium hot oil until golden brown.

Add chicken and stir quickly, then add onion and continue to stir for 30 seconds more.

Add nampla, sugar, and vinegar, then pepper and basil.

Stir quickly.

When the chicken pieces are cooked, remove immediately.

Serve with rice.

Serves 8-10.

Yum Honeymoon
(Spicy Honeymoon Eggs)

This quick and easy dish is especially for a young, newly-wed bride with limited cooking experience. It will certainly serve a dual purpose: pleasing her groom's taste buds and boosting his energy!

1 head of Boston lettuce
2 hard boiled eggs (julienne into 5 pieces)
5 red-hot peppers (julienne)
2 small purple onions (sliced)
2 tablespoons lime juice
2 tablespoons nampla (fish sauce)
2 tablespoons brown sugar
2 tablespoons dried shrimp powder

Mix sugar, nampla, and lime juice well and set aside.

Arrange lettuce leaves on a serving bowl with egg slices on top.

Top the eggs with onion slices and red peppers.

To serve, pour the lime mixture on the salad and sprinkle with the dried shrimp powder.

Serve with rice.

Serves 2.

Kài Luug Koey
(Son-in-Law Eggs)

My word of honor, I did not create this name. Let's see how yours turn out.

8 eggs (hard-boiled and peeled)
4 dried red peppers
1/2 cup bacon bits
2-4 shallots (finely sliced)
Vegetable oil for deep frying
2 tablespoons coriander leaves to garnish
4 tablespoons tamarind liquid (medium-thick)
4 tablespoons brown sugar
3 tablespoons nampla (fish sauce)
2 teaspoons chili sauce or Sambal Oelék*

On high heat, deep fry eggs until golden brown and set aside. Fry onions, dried peppers, and bacon bits—one thing at a time.

Drain and set aside.

In a sauce pan, cook chili sauce, sugar, tamarind liquid, and nampla on low heat, keep stirring until thickened.

Cut eggs into halves and arrange on a serving plate, top with bacon bits, peppers, and fried onion.

Pour hot sauce over and garnish with coriander leaves.

Serve hot with rice and other dishes.

Serves 16.

*Indonesian version of chili sauce, a substitute for Thai Sriracha (Thai chili sauce). See Glossary.

Kài Yeepun
(Japanese Eggs)

Why Japanese? No one can explain. I only know that when I was little, I was taught, or, to be exact, was programmed to like them a lot, since my mother kept telling me that they are full of all the ingredients that one needs to grow up to be a healthy person.

2-4 eggs
1-2 cups ground pork and chicken or shrimp
2 purple onions (minced)
2 medium tomatoes (diced)
1-2 tablespoons nampla (fish sauce)
1-2 tablespoons catchup
1-2 tablespoons cut-up coriander leaves
Dash of pepper
Vegetable oil to fry

Make very rare, sunny-side-up eggs and set aside.

In a pan, with 1 tablespoon vegetable oil, fry the meat with onions, nampla, and catchup. Add a little water if preferred.

When the meat is cooked, add tomato and stir to mix.

Remove from heat.

To serve, top the eggs with hot meat sauce, a dash of pepper, and garnish with coriander leaves.

Serve hot with rice.

Serves 2-4.

Ped Pad Sapparod
(Duck With Pineapple & Ginger)

The combination of plum wine, pineapple, and ginger creates an unusual and sensational dish. I hope you try this dish.

2 lbs. of thinly cut-up duck meat (bite sizes)
1 tablespoon corn flour
1/2 tablespoon brown sugar
1 1/2 tablespoons soy sauce
1/2-2/3 cup fresh ginger (thin-sliced)
2 tablespoons vegetable oil
1/2 cup of stock
1-2 cups fresh pineapple (cubes)
1 tablespoon oyster sauce
1-2 teaspoons catchup
1-2 tablespoons plum wine or white wine
1 cup sweet pepper (julienne)
1/2-2/3 cup cut-up green onions
Dash of pepper

Marinate duck meat in half of the soy sauce, sugar, and flour for at least half an hour.

In a pan, fry the duck with ginger, stock, oyster sauce, and catchup, along with the rest of the soy sauce and wine.

When the duck is done, add pepper, pineapple chunks, and green onions.

Sprinkle with black pepper before serving

Serves 4-6.

Ped Yang Siam
(Siamese Roasted Duck)

I discovered that ducks in Thailand are less fatty than in America, probably because of the way they are raised. Consequently, I boil ducks first to reduce fat. Normally, ducks need to be cooked longer than other poultry, otherwise the meat will be rather tough.

1 medium duck
4-5 stalks green onions (cut 2 stalks into 2" pieces and mince 2 teaspoons for stuffing)
4 tablespoons vinegar (1 spoon for stuffing)
3 tablespoons honey
1 tablespoon salt
1 tablespoon garlic (minced)
2 tablespoons bean sauce
1 1/2 teaspoons ginger (minced—1 teaspoon for stuffing and the rest for sauce)
4 tablespoons dark soy sauce (1 tablespoon for stuffing)
1 tablespoon Five Spices
1/2 tablespoon star anise
1-2 teaspoon fresh or dried coriander root (minced)
2-3 red-hot peppers (for sauce)

Boil duck for 10-15 minutes with cut up green onion pieces. Discard the water. Dry the duck with paper towels and set aside. Mix 1 tablespoon vinegar, honey, salt, garlic, bean sauce, ginger, green onion, 1 tablespoon dark soy sauce, Five Spices, star anise, and coriander roots. Marinate generously inside and outside the duck. Sew the duck's bottom with strong thread, let stand for at least half an hour.

Bake the duck in a 350° F. oven. Turn the duck twice during the first hour and brush it with the rest of the sauce. Lower the heat to 250° F. during the second hour, and turn the duck both sides every 15 minutes. During the last half hour, turn the heat up to broil and turn the duck on both sides. Baking time should be around 2 1/2 hours. Serve with 3 tablespoons soy sauce mixed with an equal amount of vinegar, 1/2 teaspoon of minced ginger, and 2-3 cut up red-hot peppers. Serve with rice. Serves 4.

66

Ped Toon
(Spiced Duck Stew)

For me, my mother's duck soup is the best antidote for a cold that I know, just like chicken soup for some.

1 medium duck
1-2 tablespoons soy sauce
4-5 tablespoons vegetable oil
1-2 tablespoons nampla (fish sauce)
1 star anise (roasted)
1 (1" long) piece of cinnamon (roasted)
6 fresh coriander stalks with roots (separate the leaves and mince the rest) or 1-2 teaspoons ground coriander seed
7 mushrooms
5 stalks of spring onions
Dash of pepper
Wash and cut duck (trim fat), into bite sizes (about 2-3" long). Marinate in soy sauce for 10-15 minutes.

Fry duck meat in oil until golden brown (use medium heat), then spoon the duck into a stew pot cover with 4-5 cups of water.

When the soup is boiling, add nampla and lower the heat. Then add star anise, cinnamon, and minced coriander.

When duck pieces are tender (about 1 hour), put in mushrooms and green onions.

Garnish with coriander leaves and a dash of black pepper before serving.

Serve hot with rice.

Serves 4-6.

Ped Himapan
(Duck With Cashews)

For those who love cashew nuts, this dish is delicious and very easy to fix.

2 cups duck (thinly sliced into bite-size strips)
2 teaspoons light soy sauce
4 teaspoons plum wine or white wine
3 tablespoons cornstarch
4 cloves garlic (minced)
1 purple onion (cut into 8 pieces)
3/4 cup unsalted roasted cashew nuts
5 dried red peppers (deseeded and fried)
4 stalks green onions (cut into 2" pieces)
1/3 cup vegetable oil
1 teaspoon sesame oil
2 teaspoons sugar
Dash of salt

Marinate duck pieces in soy sauce, wine, and sugar for about half an hour, then roll in cornstarch.

Heat oil and fry duck meat on medium heat until light brown, then set aside.

Fry onion and brown garlic lightly. Add nuts, peppers, and fold in the duck. Adjust to taste with sesame oil, sugar, and salt. Mix well and add green onions last.

Stir fry for 2-3 seconds more.

Serve with hot rice.

Serves 4.

Ped Palo
(Old Wife's Duck)

This soup could be kept in the freezer for as long as 9 days —in fact, the longer the better! It is quick and easy to cook and is really suitable for people who are always on the run.

1 medium duck

6 cups of stock

2 teaspoons cinnamon (or Five Spices)

1/2-1 star anise

1-2 tablespoons nampla (fish sauce)

2-3 tablespoons dark soy sauce

1/2 cup vegetable oil

1/2 tablespoon freshly ground black pepper

3 cloves garlic (minced)

1 teaspoon ginger (minced)

7-8 mushrooms (soaked in water)

5-6 stalks of green onions

5-6 minced coriander roots (save the leaves to garnish)

Roast cinnamon and star anise (one minute on high in the microwave), and mix into the stock with nampla and half of the dark soy sauce. Bring the stock to boil and set aside.

Wash duck and cut into 2" chunks and marinate in the rest of the dark soy for 5-10 minutes. Heat oil and fry duck meat on low heat until golden brown and crispy. Drop duck in the stock. Add black pepper, garlic, ginger, and coriander root.

Simmer on low heat for one hour. Add mushrooms and green onions during the last 10 minutes. Garnish with coriander leaves.

Serve hot with rice and hot sauce. Blend 1-2 cloves of garlic with 3 chili peppers, 1/2-1 teaspoon salt, and 2 tablespoons vinegar.

Serves 4-6.

Beef and Pork

Pra Ram Long Sòng
(Rama Bathing)

This is a famous classical dish from central Thailand. Pra Ram is Rama, the hero in Ramakiàn—the Thai version of the Indian Ramayana—a Hindu epic. Rama is one of the physical forms (avatars) of the God Vishnu. Because of its name and appearance, this dish is chosen to serve at both private and official ceremonies representing good fortune and happy occasions.

2-2 1/2 lbs. lean pork or shrimp or a mixture of both
4-5 dried red peppers (minced and toasted)
1/2 teaspoon salt
5 tablespoons lemon grass (minced and toasted)
1 teaspoon galanga (minced and toasted)
1 teaspoon coriander roots and leaves (minced and toasted)
3 tablespoons garlic (minced)
4 tablespoons shallots (minced)
4 tablespoons ground peanuts (roasted)
1/4 teaspoon ground turmeric—optional
1/2 teaspoon shrimp paste—optional

4 tablespoons brown sugar
5 tablespoons nampla (fish sauce)
1 lb. fresh spinach (cleaned)
6 1/2 tablespoons medium-thick coconut milk
1/2 cup of coconut cream—optional

Blend dried peppers into a paste with salt. Add lemon grass, galanga, coriander, garlic, shallots, shrimp paste, turmeric (if used), and peanuts. Simmer pork (if used), in coconut milk. Add the paste mixture and continue to simmer until the oil separates. If you use shrimp, add them at this point and adjust the taste with sugar and nampla. Boil spinach quickly. Drain and arrange in a ring on a serving platter. Spoon pork (or shrimp) and sauce into the center. Then beat the coconut cream (if used), until frothy and spoon over spinach to make the foam of the sea of emerald water where Rama is bathing. I have used this as one dish meal, arrange rice in the plate. Place spinach on the rice, and top with meat and shrimp. Serves 8.

Seu Rong Hai
(Weeping Tiger Beef)

The story goes like this. Once there was a hunter who had just finished consuming his creation—this beef dish—and went to sleep (in his tree house, of course). Suddenly, he was awakened by a strange noise—a tiger weeping in dismay! The grief-stricken tiger had followed the aroma of the beef just to find there was not a single piece left for him. It is up to you to prove this dish. From the story, you can easily guess that it originated from the northeastern part of Thailand.

2 lbs. flank beef
1 tablespoon soy sauce
1-2 tablespoons white sesame seeds—optional
2 tablespoons cooking wine, brandy, or Mekong whisky*
1-2 teaspoons of brown sugar
1-2 teaspoons of salt
2-3 tablespoons low-fat margarine or frying oil
1 tablespoon nampla (fish sauce)

Ingredients for sauce:

2 red-hot peppers (minced)
Juice of 1 lime
2 cloves garlic (minced)
2 tablespoons brown sugar

Slice meat thinly into 2" pieces. Marinate in soy sauce, salt, sugar, wine, and nampla sprinkle with sesame seeds and set aside for at least 15-30 minutes. Lay the meat in pan and bake on low heat until dried (about 15 minutes). Heat oil or margarine and fry meat on high heat until brown on both sides. You can also barbeque the meat, or just fry on medium heat for 2-3 minutes each side and drain oil well.

Serve with the sauce, made by mixing: minced red peppers, juice of one lime, minced garlic, and brown sugar. Serves 8-10.

*Thai whiskey

Gang Hunglay
(Hunglay Curry)

This dish is influenced by Burmese curry. The northern people of Thailand adapted it to suit their tastes. Red-hot peppers, shrimp paste, lemon grass, and nampla are Thai favorite ingredients. The bright red color of the peppers and the yellow color of turmeric will create the beautiful orange shade of this curry.

2 1/2 lbs. beef, pork, or chicken (cut into 2" cubes)
2-3 tablespoons dark soy sauce
5 dried red peppers
1-2 stalks of lemon grass (minced)
1/2 cup peeled pearl onions or purple onions (cut up)
1/2 cup peeled garlic (crushed)
1/2 tablespoon shrimp paste
1 teaspoon salt
1/2-1 teaspoon turmeric (or curry powder)
1/2-1 cup thick tamarind liquid
1/2 cup ginger (minced)

2 tablespoons nampla and brown sugar (to taste)
1-2 cups fresh pineapple, mango or substitute Mango Chutney (cut up into 2" pieces)
1/2 cup of roasted peanuts—optional
5 cups of water

Marinate meat in soy sauce for about 15 minutes. In a blender, or food processor, mix peppers, lemon grass, onion, garlic, shrimp paste, salt, and turmeric or curry powder until smooth.

Boil water in a pot to cook meat with the curry paste, keep the curry on low heat until the meat is tender. Then, add the tamarind liquid and continue to simmer while adding ginger, sugar, and nampla to taste. Before removing the pot from the heat, drop in the pineapple or mango pieces (or mango chutney), and peanuts (if used). Stir and serve.

Serve hot with rice. Serves 6-8.

Stew Nam Kon
(Special Beef Stew)

This is my mother's famous stew that I missed so terribly when I first left home to study in the States. I could say that this dish gave me the reason to learn to cook. Try it and see if you would feel the same as I did!

2 lbs. flank beef (2" x 2" pieces)
10-12 strips of bacon (roll into balls)
1 (12 oz.) can of evaporated milk
3/4 tablespoon salt
4-5 onions (cut up)
4-6 potatoes (boiled, peeled, and cut in half)
1 crushed nutmeg or about 1 teaspoon ground
1 1/2 teaspoons mace
5-7 whole cardamoms
5-6 cloves
1 (3") stick cinnamon
2/3 cup Worcestershire sauce
Vegetable oil to fry

Make a hole in each beef chunk and stuff it with a bacon roll.

In a big frying pan, heat oil on medium high and fry the beef chunks until golden brown on all sides.

Spoon the beef chunks into a stew pot, with water just to cover the beef. Bring the soup to boil. Add potatoes, onions, and salt to the soup.

While boiling, gradually pour in milk. Add nutmeg, mace, cardamom, cloves, and cinnamon stick. Lower the heat to between medium and simmer. Add Worcestershire sauce.

Continue to cook for at least an hour, or until the meat is tender. Serve with rice or bread.

Serves 4-6.

Mòo Pad Kïng
(Pork with Ginger)

You can make a vegetarian dish with this recipe by substituting tofu for the meat—use the same amount. If served with rice, it can be a tasty and satisfying one-dish meal. Mòo Pad Kïng is from central Thailand.

2 cups lean pork, chicken, or flank beef (cut up into 2" pieces)
1 teaspoon minced garlic
1 tablespoon onion (sliced)
1/4 cup white bean sauce
1/2-1 cup ginger (1/10 lb. slivered)
2-3 tablespoons soy sauce
2 tablespoons brown sugar
1 tablespoon vinegar
2 cups mushrooms—hed hunu or Chinese mushrooms (soaked in water for 10-15 minutes)
2-3 tablespoons nampla (fish sauce)
8 tablespoons stock—optional
1/4 cup red chili peppers (slivered)
2-3 spring onions (cut into 2" pieces)
1/3 cup vegetable oil to fry
Dash of white pepper

Heat oil in a big pan and fry onion and garlic.

Add pork. When pork is cooked, add bean sauce, ginger, soy sauce, sugar, vinegar, mushrooms, and nampla. Add some stock (if used), or water. Stir well.

Add pepper, spring onions, and a dash of white pepper before serving.

Serves 8.

Mòo Wan
(Sweet Pork)

Mòo Wan is good with rice soup for breakfast (central Thai style). You can also add it to your fried rice or a dried noodle dish.

2 lbs. pork loin (cut up in bite sizes)
2 cups purple onions (sliced)
1 cup water
1/4 cup nampla (fish sauce)
2-4 tablespoons brown sugar
1/4 cup garlic (minced)
1/2 cup coriander roots and leaves (cut up)
1 head of red lettuce
2-4 tablespoons vegetable oil to fry

Mix water, nampla and sugar. Set aside. Blend coriander and garlic.

Heat pan with oil and fry the garlic mixture then add pork, onion, and the salty-sweet liquid.

Stir fry until it is thickened (to your taste).

Arrange pork with the red lettuce leaves.

Serves 6-8.

Mara Sod Sâi
(Pork in Sleeping Bag)

This is another way to create a delicious soup from a bitter melon. People from central Thailand tend to take time to create their food to look interesting and decorative, as well as taste delicious.

2 bitter melons
1 1/2 cups lean ground pork
3/4 cup of fresh shrimp—optional (cut up)
1-2 coriander leaves and roots (separate leaves)
5 cloves garlic
1/4 teaspoon black pepper
1-2 tablespoons nampla (fish sauce)
6-12 Chinese mushrooms,hed hunu, or wood fungus (minced)
6-7 cups stock or water
3 tablespoons soy sauce
6 teaspoons cut-up preserved cabbages or mustard greens

Cut the melons in half—about 2 1/2" long. Spoon out the seeds and soak in warm, salty water about 15 minutes.

Blend coriander, garlic, and pepper. Mix in nampla and fold into the ground pork and shrimp (if used). Mix in the mushrooms. Spoon the mixture into the melon pieces.

Drop the melon pieces into a large pot of boiling water or stock with soy sauce. Cook on medium heat about 45 minutes. Do not stir.

In a serving bowl, top the soup with preserved cabbage pieces and coriander leaves.

Serve hot.

Serves 6-8.

Gang Ped Chow Rai
(Banana Red Curry)

Chow Rai means farmer. They grow almost all the ingredients for their food. One fruit that is indispensable is the banana.

2 1/2-3 lbs. flank beef (cut into bite sizes)
6 cups medium-thin and 3/4 cup thick coconut milk
4-5 unripened bananas (cut into 1/2" pieces, soak in water)
6-9 young chili peppers (slivered)
2/3 cup of fresh sweet basil
1/4 cup brown sugar
1/2 teaspoon kaffir lime leaves
1/4 cup nampla (fish sauce)
2 teaspoons galanga
9 dried red peppers
2 tablespoons lemon grass (minced)
9 cloves garlic (minced)
10 pearl onions or tiny purple onions (minced)
1 tablespoon coriander seeds or fresh with roots
1 teaspoon cumin
12 whole black peppers
1/4 teaspoon nutmeg
1/2 teaspoon mace
1 tablespoon shrimp paste

Blend the last 11 ingredients (from galanga to shrimp paste) until smooth.

Cook beef pieces in 2 cups of coconut milk slowly, use medium heat until almost liquefied.

Fry curry paste in half of the thick coconut milk until fragrant, then mix into the pot with the beef. Mix in the rest of coconut milk. Adjust to taste with nampla. Add banana, kaffir leaves, and sugar. Top with the rest of the thick coconut milk, young peppers (slivered), and sweet basil before serving.

Serve with plain rice. Serves 14-16.

Tom Mòo Sapparod
(Crispy Pork with Pineapple)

These flavors will be familiar to many who have eaten oriental dishes.

3 cups lean pork (cut up)
8 stalks coriander leaves and roots (washed and cut up)
1-2 teaspoons black pepper
3 tablespoons minced onions
1 teaspoon shrimp paste
2 tablespoons dried fish (or anchovy powder)
8 cups water
1 pineapple (cut up)
5 tablespoons nampla (fish sauce)
5 tablespoons brown sugar
4-5 tablespoons tamarind liquid
2 teaspoons salt
vegetable oil for frying

Fry pork pieces (slightly coated in salt) in 1/4 cup of vegetable oil until light brown.

Blend coriander, onion, pepper, shrimp paste, and dried fish powder (used some water).

Boil water in a soup pot, mix in the paste.

While the soup is boiling, drop the meat in with tamarind liquid, nampla, sugar, and pineapple last.

Serve hot with rice.

Serves 12.

Tom Klong
(Pork Mango Stew)

2 1/2 cups lean pork or chicken breast (cut up in bite sizes)
8-10 cups water
1-2 teaspoons galanga (1" long)
3-5 roasted dried red peppers
3 lemon grasses (cracked and cut into 2" long pieces)
2 teaspoons kaffir lime leaves
3 onions (cracked)
5-6 tablespoons green mango or green apple (slivered)
4 tablespoons nampla (fish sauce)
7-8 stalks of coriander leaves
1-2 limes
3 fresh hot peppers—optional

Boil pork or chicken on low heat with galanga, dried red peppers, lemon grass, kaffir leaves, onion, and green mango.

When the meat is done, season with nampla and lime juice.

Garnish with coriander leaves and fresh peppers.

Serves 10-12.

Mòo Kam Wan
(Sweet-Golden Pork)

2 1/2 lbs. lean pork (cut into bite-sized pieces)

1 1/2 tablespoons light soy sauce

2 tablespoons oyster sauce

2 tablespoons nampla (fish sauce)

2 tablespoons honey

2 tablespoons white wine

1 1/2 tablespoons sesame oil

1 teaspoon ground pepper

Fresh vegetable of choice (lettuce, spinach or endive)

Ingredients for sauce:

1 red-hot pepper

4-5 coriander roots and leaves

1 teaspoon minced garlic

3 tablespoons brown sugar

3 tablespoons lime juice

1 tablespoon nampla (fish sauce)

Place the pork pieces in a mixture of soy sauce, oyster sauce, nampla, honey, white wine, sesame oil, and ground pepper. Marinate all night (if you have time). Fry them on low heat until golden brown (no oil necessary).

To make sauce: Crush pepper with garlic and coriander roots (separate the leaves and set aside). Mix in nampla, lime juice, and sugar. Garnish the sauce with coriander leaves.

To serve, wrap meat in vegetable leaves and dip into the sauce.

Serve with rice.

Serves 4.

Makeu Sod Sâi
(Stuffed Eggplant)

This dish will add a beautiful touch to your table. It is rather hot and tasty. Eggplant can help tone down the spiciness. You can also use sweet or Mexican finger peppers to garnish.

1 green or purple eggplant
1 cup lean ground pork and minced shrimp
2 teaspoons minced garlic
3 tablespoons purple onion (minced)
1-2 teaspoons ground red pepper
1-2 teaspoons ground coriander seed or fresh roots
1 tablespoon nampla (fish sauce)
1 tablespoon brown sugar
1/2 cup basil leaves
1-2 red and yellow hot peppers (julienne)
Vegetable oil to fry
Vegetables of choice (lettuce, carrot, cucumber)

On medium heat, fry eggplant in vegetable oil until done on all sides and cut into halves.

Spoon out the seeds and a little part of the inside. Set aside.

Heat oil and fry garlic and onion with ground red pepper, and coriander seed. Add pork, nampla, and sugar, then shrimp and basil leaves. Spoon the cooked ingredients into the eggplant halves.

Garnish with red and yellow peppers.

Arrange vegetables around the dish and serve with rice

Serves 4.

Seafood

Tom Yum Gung
(Shrimp Lemon Grass Soup)

This is one of the most famous Thai dishes. Most visitors to the country have tried it. Almost every Thai restaurant, both in Thailand and abroad, has this dish on its menu. It originated in central Thailand. Try and see if it deserves to be well-known.

6 cups of water
6 pieces of (2-3") fresh lemon grass
1 lb. shrimp (peeled and deveined)
4-6 scallions (thinly sliced)
6-8 mushrooms
6 kaffir lime leaves (fresh preferred)
5 tablespoons nampla
3 big limes (about 3/4 cup of lime juice)
1-2 hot chili peppers (seeded and julienne)
2 tablespoons cut up coriander (cilantro) leaves

Boil water, add lemon grass, shrimp, scallions, mushrooms, and kaffir leaves.

Add nampla, lime juice, and chili peppers, last.

Simmer with lid on for about 10-15 minutes.

Adjust to taste. Garnish with coriander leaves before serving.

Serves 4-6.

Gung Kratiem
(Garlic Fried Shrimp)

Among all the seafood, I like shrimp most. There is no end to ways of cooking shrimp in Thai cuisine. This dish is my favorite and also one of the easiest ways to prepare shrimp.

This recipe can be used with squid or pork

1 lb. large shrimp (cleaned, deveined, and sprinkled with salt and vinegar)
1/4 cup vegetable oil
1 tablespoon of garlic (chopped)
1 teaspoon nampla (fish sauce)
1 large lime
1 teaspoon of Maggi sauce
1-2 teaspoons of Chinese white bean sauce
6 stalks of coriander leaves (cut up)
1/2 teaspoon sesame oil
Dash of black pepper and sugar (to taste)

Heat oil and cook garlic to light golden brown. Add shrimp and nampla. Cook for one minute or less.

Remove shrimp, then squeeze juice of 1/2 lime and Maggi sauce onto the shrimp. Top the shrimp with coriander leaves.

Put the rest of the lime juice, pepper, bean sauce, sesame oil, and a dash of sugar in the pan. Cook and stir about half a minute.

Pour the sauce from the frying pan on the shrimp before serving.

Add the mushrooms to the sauce before removing from heat.

Serve with hot rice. Serves 6-8.

Gang Kua Sapparod Gung
(Pineapple Shrimp Curry)

This style of curry is from the central region. You could use young pickled bamboo shoots instead of pineapple. The taste is different. I like it both ways.

1/2-1 cup fresh shrimp (peeled and deveined)

3 dried red-hot peppers (soaked in water)

1-2 tablespoons lemon grass (minced and roasted)

1-2 tablespoons galanga (roasted)

4 teaspoons onion (minced and roasted)

1/2 teaspoon shrimp paste

1/2 teaspoon salt

3 tablespoons dried shrimp powder

2 1/2 cups medium-thin coconut milk

1 pineapple or 2 cups canned chunk pineapple

2-3 tablespoons nampla (fish sauce)

1 teaspoon brown sugar (or to taste)

4 teaspoons garlic (minced and roasted)

2 tablespoons tamarind liquid

Blend red peppers, lemon grass, galanga, onion, shrimp paste, salt, garlic, and dried shrimp powder into a paste.

Heat a pan to boil the coconut milk and gradually add the curry paste. Stir well.

Cut the pineapple into bite sizes and add to the mixture. Then, add nampla, tamarind liquid, and sugar. Adjust the taste. Put in the shrimps last.

When shrimps are cooked, serve with rice.

Serves 4-6.

Gang Om Mara
(Bitter Melon Curry)

The word "Om," from northern Thailand, means slow cooking. After you drop the fish in the curry pot, you should lower the heat. This way, the meat and the melon pieces will absorb the juice of the curry, which results in a more tasty dish.

1 1/4 lbs. fish fillets or chicken breast (cut up)
1 bitter melon (sliced and soaked in salted water)
1/2 cup thick and 4 cups thin coconut milk
5 dried red peppers
2 tablespoons lemon grass (minced)
1 teaspoon kaffir lime leaves (minced)
9 black peppers
5 scallions (sliced)
2 cloves garlic (minced)
5 slices of galanga
1 crispy dried fish or dried anchovy—optional
1 teaspoon shrimp paste
2 teaspoons roasted coriander seed
A few stalks of coriander
Coriander leaves (to garnish)
3-4 tablespoons nampla (fish sauce)
1-2 teaspoons brown sugar

Blend red peppers, coriander stalks and seed, lemon grass, kaffir lime leaves, black peppers, scallions, garlic, galanga, dried fish, and shrimp paste into a paste.

Heat a pan with 3 tablespoons of thick coconut milk. Fry the paste, nampla, and sugar, then add 4 cups of thin coconut milk. When the mixture is boiling, drop the fish in and spoon the bitter melon pieces from the salty water. Then, drain and rinse them well. Add to the curry last. Do not stir. Keep cooking on low heat. Top the curry with thick coconut milk before serving. Garnish with coriander leaves.

Serve with rice or Thai rice noodles. Serves 6-8.

Pôo Jaa
(Spicy Crab Cake)

Pôo Jaa is a creation of the central region. You could put the crab mixture in canapé shells or other fancy containers to help beautify your dining table.

1 cup shrimp (minced)
1 cup crabmeat
1 cup ground pork (lean)
1/2 cup mashed potato or taro
3-4 roots and stalks of coriander (separate leaves—minced)
3-4 cloves garlic (minced)
1/2 teaspoon black pepper
1 teaspoon green onion (minced)
16 slivers of green and red peppers (to garnish)
1 egg (beaten)
1 tablespoon soy sauce
2 tablespoons nampla (fish sauce)
dash of sugar

Mix garlic, roots and stalks of coriander, pepper, soy sauce, egg, sugar, nampla, and green onion. Then fold in crab, pork, shrimp and potato.

Fry a bite of the mixture and sample the taste. Spoon the mixture into small cups (canapé shells) and garnish with coriander leaves, and red and green pepper slivers.

Steam them about 20 minutes.

Serve hot with Sriracha sauce.

Serves 8-12.

Tod Man Pla
(Spicy Fish Cake)

This dish can be served as an appetizer or with the main dish. It is very popular, especially in Bangkok, where you can find it at street-corner stalls and in top restaurants.

2 cups of firm, fresh, skinless fillets of fish (feather-back fish, cod, haddock, or monkfish)

4 dried red peppers (deseeded)

10-12 black peppers

3/4 teaspoon salt

1 tablespoon coriander roots and stalks (minced)

1 tablespoon lemon grass (minced)

1 1/2 tablespoons garlic (minced)

1 tablespoon pearl onion (minced)

1/2-1 teaspoon ground galanga

1-2 eggs or just egg whites—optional

2 cups green beans or sweet beans or winged beans (minced)

1 1/2 tablespoons nampla

3-4 kaffir lime leaves (slivered finely)

Vegetable oil to deep fry

Ingredients for the cucumber relish:

1 big cucumber (sliced thinly)

1-2 tablespoons ground roasted peanuts

4 tablespoons rice vinegar

5 tablespoons sugar

1/2-1 teaspoon salt

1-2 red peppers (slivered)

Blend black and red peppers, salt, coriander, lemon grass, garlic, onion, and galanga into a paste. Mash the fillet in a mortar or food processor. Roll into the paste and knead. Mix the dough with eggs, bean, nampla, and kaffir lime leaves. Form the fish dough into a 2" x 2" round sheets. Heat oil in deep pan, fry the fish patties on medium heat until golden brown—2-3 minutes. Serve with cucumber relish. To make the cucumber relish: Mix the last 4 ingredients and roll in the cucumber slices. Top with peanuts. To serve, top the fish cake with the relish. Serves 8-10.

Tom Yum Pla
(Fish in Coconut Milk)

You could use chicken breast in place of the fish for this recipe. In that case, there is no need to rinse off the salt and vinegar from the chicken breast.

1 lb. red snapper (cut in bite sizes)

1 teaspoon salt and vinegar

2 1/2 cups thin and 1 cup thick coconut milk

2-3 teaspoons tamarind paste

2-3 stalks lemon grass or 1 tablespoon dried lemon grass powder

5 kaffir lime leaves

1-2 tablespoons nampla (fish sauce)

1/2 cup lime juice

2 scallions (cut into 1" pieces)

1 teaspoon chili pepper (chopped)

2-3 coriander leaves (for garnish)

Dash of sugar—optional

Sprinkle fish with salt and vinegar and rinse off. In a sauce pan, boil 2 1/2 cups of thin coconut milk with tamarind paste, then add lemon grass, kaffir lime leaves, nampla, and half of the lime juice. Then add the fish all at once.

Do not stir.

Boil for 5 minutes, then add thick coconut milk, stir, and bring to boil. Then, remove immediately.

When you are ready to serve, add the rest of the lime juice (to taste), chopped chili, scallions, more nampla, and a dash of sugar, if you like.

Garnish with coriander leaves before serving.

Serves 6-8.

Tom Kha Gung Kâo Pod
(Galanga Shrimp with Corn)

If you use chicken to cook this dish, without corn, but with onion, cumin, and cinnamon, you might recognize its twin as an Indonesian dish called "Opor Ayam." I have no idea which one was born first. This one was born in central Thailand, though.

1 lb. medium shrimp or chicken breasts (peeled and deveined)
6 cups medium-thin coconut milk
5 stalks crushed lemon grass (cut into 1" pieces and using only white parts)
8 sliced fresh or dried galanga
1 teaspoon ginger (minced)
6 kaffir leaves
1 lb. young corn
1/2 cup nampla (fish sauce)
10 tablespoons lime juice or tamarind liquid
4-5 stalks coriander
10 fresh peppers (slivered)
Dash of black pepper

Boil coconut milk and put in stalks of lemon grass, galanga pieces, ginger, kaffir leaves, and corn.

Drop in the shrimp and let boil for about 10-15 seconds.

Remove from heat. Add nampla, lime juice, coriander leaves, and a dash of fresh pepper before serving.
Serve hot with rice.

Serves 16.

91

Pla Op King
(Steamed Fish with Ginger)

In Isan (northeastern Thailand), after a successful day of fishing, people just make a fire near the bank of the Mekong River to barbeque their catch. They use banana leaves to wrap the fish and have a big feast right there in the moonlight. It is extremely tasty in such an atmosphere. With your imagination and aluminum foil (instead of banana leaves), you could create the same taste in your own home.

3 lbs. fresh fish fillets
1/4 cup fresh ginger root (peeled and slivered)
2 limes
1/4 teaspoon each of ground pepper and salt
3 spring onions (minced, separating white and green part)
1/4 cup vegetable oil
1 tablespoon sesame oil
6-10 cloves garlic (sliced finely)
4-6 tablespoons sesame seeds

5 tablespoons Kikkoman or soy sauce
1 teaspoon powdered lemon grass
2-3 stalks of fresh coriander (cut up)
1-2 red peppers (slivered)
Aluminum foil (in place of banana leaves)

Sprinkle the fish fillets with salt and pepper and set aside. Marinate ginger in lime juice, then heat oil to fry garlic to light brown. Pour garlic and oil over ginger. Fry sesame seeds until golden brown. Blend into the mixture of garlic and ginger, then add white part of minced, spring onions, lemon grass and soy sauce, last. Mix the sauce well and sprinkle generously over the fillets of fish. Top each piece of fish with sesame oil and coriander. Wrap each of the fillets in foil and steam about 15 minutes. Garnish with slivered red peppers and the green part of minced spring onions.

Serve hot with rice and with more lime juice. Serves 8-10.

Pla Jiean
(Dressed-Up Fish)

This typical Thai way of cooking fish is from among the recipes that my mother sent to save my life while I was a student in the States. The word "jiean" is the special way of cooking with ginger included in the four tastes normally found in Thai cuisine (sweet, sour, salty, and hot).

1 fish (3 lbs.) or fillet (sea bass, snapper, mackerel, dollar fish, or butter fish)
1 1/2 tablespoons onion (minced)
1/4 cup ginger (minced)
2 tablespoons nampla (fish sauce)
2 tablespoons brown sugar
2 tablespoons tamarind liquid
3 stalks of green onions
2-3 stalks of coriander
2-3 red peppers (slivered)
Vegetable oil to deep fry
Few drops of lime juice or vinegar

In a frying pan with vegetable oil, drop vinegar or lime juice. Heat the oil and fry the fish until light brown and crispy.

Drain the oil and set aside.

Fry minced onion until golden. Add ginger and stir for a few seconds, then add nampla, sugar, and tamarind liquid. If it is too dry, add a little water.

Drop in cut-up green onions and gently mix the ingredients.

Remove from the heat and pour the mixture over the fish.

Garnish with coriander leaves and slivered red peppers. Serve hot with rice.

Serves 2-4.

Gung Saam Ros
(Triple Tastes Prawn)

This is one of my favorite Bangkok delicacies. You could arrange colorful vegetables, such as radish, carrot, and endive, around the shrimp or on the side of the dish to create a beautiful dish.

1 1/2 lbs. (48-50) medium sized prawns (deveined)
6-7 red and green hot peppers or 2-3 sweet peppers
1/2 teaspoon salt
1/2 teaspoon galanga
1/2 teaspoon coriander roots (or ground)
9 black peppercorns
2 teaspoons garlic (minced)
1 tablespoon purple onion (minced)
1/3 cup tamarind liquid
2 tablespoons brown sugar
1 1/2 tablespoons nampla
1/2 cup of vegetable oil or Pam non-stick cooking spray
Vegetables of your choice

Spray Pam (non-stick cooking spray) on pan and fry shrimp on medium-high heat quickly (to golden brown), then spoon into a serving dish.

Blend all the ingredients until coarsely smooth, then, fry in 1/2 cup of vegetable oil.

Pour the fried sauce over the shrimp.

Serve hot with rice.

Serves 6-8.

Sukothai Steam Fish
(Northern Style Fish)

The northern region has a delicate way of cooking fish which has a refined and milder taste than other regions. This simple dish is worth trying.

1 1/2 lbs. fresh fish fillet

2 cups water

2 teaspoons garlic (minced)

3 teaspoons salt

3 tablespoons lemon grass (minced)

2 teaspoons turmeric

3-6 green chili peppers

Blend peppers, turmeric, lemon grass, salt, and garlic until smooth.

Add this mixture to pot with 2 cups of water and stir well.

Heat to boiling. Then drop in fish fillets to cook over medium heat.

Cover the pot and let the fish absorb the sauce.

Serve with rice.

Serves 6-8.

Pla Lerd Ros
(Superb Fish)

This spicy and delicious dish is a creation of the central part of Thailand—probably from Bangkok. The degree of hotness depends on the number and variety of chili peppers you choose (see glossary).

1 lb. of mackerel, whiting, sea bass, or silver pomfret
1-2 teaspoons flour
Dash of salt
2 1/2 tablespoons vegetable oil
10 black peppers
2 teaspoons purple onion or 6 shallots—minced
2 teaspoons garlic—minced
4-7 hot chili peppers (sliver one for garnish and chop the rest for the paste)
3-4 stalks coriander or ground seed and a few leaves for garnishing
1/2 teaspoon minced or ground galanga—optional
2 1/2 tablespoons stock—optional
2/3 cup tamarind liquid or 2 1/2 tablespoons lime juice
2 tablespoons nampla or to taste
2-3 tablespoons brown sugar
1 head lettuce

Wash fish and roll in the mixture of flour and salt. Heat oil in pan and fry fish until crispy brown on both sides.

Arrange the fish in a bed of lettuce leaves and set aside.

Blend peppers, onion, garlic, chili, coriander roots, and galanga into a paste. Fry the paste with stock, tamarind liquid, nampla and sugar. Stir until thickened and pour over the fish.

Garnish with coriander leaves and slivered red chili pepper.

Serve with rice.

Serves 2-4.

More than half of the recipes in this section are from the central part of the country. The area, in and around Bangkok, is full of canals. Any visitor who has spent time at the floating markets can confirm that there is no end to Thai fresh-water fish and seafood, including lobsters, crabs, and shellfish. These products are very inexpensive in Thailand, compared to America, and they are prepared to please your taste buds.

Haw Mok Talay
(Seafood Steam Pot)

Haw Mok means "wrap up a surprise." Each part of Thailand has this style of cooking, though the taste and ways to prepare are somehow different. The people of central Thailand also use pork and chicken in Haw Mok, besides fresh water fish, seafood, and fish eggs. In Bangkok, there are many original and interesting ways to present this dish, such as steaming in a young coconut. The vegetables used are also different according to the region. This recipe is an example of Bangkok Haw Mok.

3 lbs. of seafood (crab meat, mussels, shrimp, red snapper, scallops, etc.)
3 tablespoons fresh or dried lemon grass (minced)
3 tablespoons garlic (minced)
3 tablespoons onion (minced)
3 teaspoons ground galanga (3-4 thin slices)
1 tablespoon coriander seed or fresh roots
1 teaspoon nutmeg

1 teaspoon rhizome
7-10 dried red peppers (soak and remove the seeds)
1 teaspoon salt
1 teaspoon shrimp paste
1 teaspoon sugar—optional
2 teaspoons fresh kaffir lime leaves (slivered)
3 tablespoons nampla (fish sauce)
1 egg—optional
3 cups of medium-thick coconut milk
1/2 cup thick coconut milk
1 teaspoon rice flour
15-20 basil leaves
3 fresh red peppers (slivered)
1 cup of vegetable (cabbage, endive, or collard greens)

Blend lemon grass, garlic, onion, galanga, coriander, nutmeg, rhizome, pepper, salt, shrimp paste, and sugar (if used), until smooth.

98

Haw Mok Talay cont...
(Seafood Steam Pot)

Remove the paste to a bowl.

Add coconut milk gradually while stirring with a wooden spoon.

Mix well and add seafood, nampla, and egg to the mixture.

Keep on stirring until the mixture becomes sticky.

In a steaming pot—small individual pots or one large one—arrange vegetable leaves on the bottom and spoon the mixture into the pot.

Steam for 15-20 minutes (covered).

Mix thick coconut milk with a dash of salt and rice flour.

Cook on low heat.

Top the pot with the cooked coconut milk and garnish with red peppers, kaffir lime, and basil leaves.

Continue to steam for few minutes more.

Remove from heat and serve with rice.

Serves 8-10.

Tom Sôm Talay
(Seafood Sour Soup)

This seafood hot pot was created in the central Thailand. There is no limit to the variety of seafood that you can add. As for myself, I love crab meat and squid. Mussels and clams will also add pleasant touch to the soup.

1 1/2 cups shrimp, fish, and scallops
5-6 cups of water
7 dried red peppers (soaked)
1 teaspoon salt
3 tablespoons onion (sliced)
1 1/2 tablespoons garlic (minced)
1/2-1 teaspoon shrimp paste
1 teaspoon galanga
1 1/2 teaspoons cut up coriander leaves
1/2 teaspoon black pepper
2 tablespoons nampla (fish sauce)
2 tablespoons tamarind paste
2 tablespoons brown sugar

2 1/2 cups selected vegetables (green beans, baby corn, cabbage, broccoli, spinach, or pineapple etc.)

Blend dried red peppers, salt, onion, garlic, shrimp paste, galanga, coriander, and black pepper into a paste.

In a pot, boil 5 cups of water and nampla. Put in fish and scallops. Mix in tamarind paste and sugar, and then the shrimp and selected vegetables.

Serve hot.

Serves 6-8.

Pla Dug Foo
(Puffy Catfish with Mango Sauce)

Pla Dug Foo is my husband's most favorite Thai dish, and I agree with him. I bet you will, too.

1 catfish (cleaned and barbequed)

2/3 cup vegetable oil to fry

1 green mango (peeled and slivered)

9-10 pearl onions (sliced thinly)

3 tablespoons lime juice

5 dried red peppers (roasted and cut up)

1 1/2 tablespoons nampla (fish sauce)

1 tablespoon brown sugar

1-2 fresh red-hot peppers—optional (julienne)

7-8 cloves garlic (minced)

2-4 stalks coriander leaves

1/2 cup dried roasted peanuts (unsalted)

Few drops of vinegar

10 lettuce leaves

Barbeque fish, then skin and debone it. Use fork to puff up the fish meat.

In pan, heat oil and drop vinegar into the oil, deep fry fish until golden crisp. Spoon the fish on to a paper towel to drain.

Arrange lettuce leaves on a serving plate, spoon the fish to top the leaves, and garnish with dry roasted peanuts.

Blend garlic with dried red peppers and mix sauce with lime juice, nampla, and sugar. Mix in mango and onion, and top with red peppers (if used), and coriander leaves.

To serve, spoon the mango sauce on the fish and lettuce.

Serve with rice.

Serves 2-4.

Pad Ped Pla Lai
(Hot Eel)

This dish is considered a traditional dish among the unconventional Thais. It can also be served as a spicy hors d'oeuvre with drinks before dinner.

1 1/4 lbs. eel (clean with salt, cut in half to debone and cut into bite-sizes. Soak eel pieces in wine and set aside)
7 dried red peppers (coreless)
1-2 tablespoons coriander seed and 3-4 stalks of fresh coriander (roast the seed)
1 teaspoon whole black peppers (roasted and crushed)
1 teaspoon cumin (roasted)
3 small cloves garlic (crushed)
1 small purple onion (cut up)
20 fresh peppercorns—optional
1 teaspoon galanga
1 stalk lemon grass (crushed and cut up)
1 teaspoon kaffir lime leaves
1 cup holy basil
1/4 cup rhizome

1 teaspoon shrimp paste
1/2 cup vegetable oil
Dash of salt
6-7 red peppers (julienne)
2-3 tablespoons nampla (fish sauce)
Dash of brown sugar (to taste)

Blend dried red peppers, and peppercorns, coriander seed, black peppers, cumin, garlic, onion, galanga, lemon grass, rhizome, shrimp paste, and salt into a paste.

Fry the paste in oil until fragrant, then drop in the eel pieces, nampla, and sugar. Add basil, kaffir lime leaves, julienne red pepper, and fresh peppercorns.

Stir fry quickly. When the eel is done, remove from heat and garnish with coriander leaves.

Serve hot with rice. Serves 4-6.

Gung Ten
(Dancing Prawn)

This is my mother's specialty. After the first bite, you might want to argue that it is not only the prawn that dances alone, the consumer can not refrain from jumping too. If you are too scared of the Prík Kee Nùu, you could use a milder kind of pepper and add sugar to the dish. It might help. Good luck!

1 1/4 lbs. of fresh prawns
10 cloves garlic (crushed and minced)
5-7 green and red-hot peppers—Prík Kee Nùu preferred (minced)
3-4 tablespoons lime juice
3-4 tablespoons nampla
1/2 cup of fresh mint
2 tablespoons lemon grass using only very white parts (finely minced)
1 tablespoon white sugar—optional
1 tablespoon coriander leaves
10-20 leaves of iceberg or romaine lettuce

Arrange the lettuce leaves on a serving plate.

Barbeque the prawn quickly.

Slice length-wise to top the lettuce leaves.

Top the prawns with minced garlic, mint, lemon grass, peppers, and coriander leaves. Just before serving, add lime juice, nampla, and sugar (if used).

Toss and serve.

Serves 4-6.

Rice and Noodle Dishes

The first time I went to a Thai restaurant in America, I felt empathy for non-Thais who tried their best to eat with chopsticks, especially to pick every kernel of rice from a flat container. Most seemed to think that all Asians eat with chopsticks and had requested them from the obliging waiters. At the same time, the Thai customers were happily eating with spoons and forks, as is the Thai custom! It is true that Chinese eat everything with chopsticks, but they have rice in small bowls and lift the bowls up, using chopsticks to help pushing rice into their mouths.

Pad Thai
(Thai Fried Noodle)

This is the most famous Thai fried noodle dish, a creation of central Thailand. You have to try it to find out why it is renowned. You can also serve this as one main dish (for lunch) or with rice and some other dishes at dinner.

8 oz. rice noodle (softened in cold water)
1 lb. lean pork or chicken (cut up in 1" pieces)
1/4 cup medium deveined shrimp or dried shrimp powder)
1/4-1/2 cup crushed peanuts
2 tablespoons pickled mustard greens, radish, or pickled garlic, and sliced celery—optional (chopped)
1/4 lb. tofu
1-2 fresh tomatoes or 1 tablespoon tomato paste
2-3 tablespoons nampla (fish sauce)
2-3 tablespoons brown sugar
1 tablespoon tamarind liquid or vinegar
2 tablespoons garlic (minced)
1 tablespoon onions (minced)
1 tablespoon soy bean sauce

4 tablespoons vegetable oil
1-2 eggs—optional
1-2 cups bean sprouts
4-5 coriander leaves
2-3 limes (slices)
1-2 tablespoons catchup—optional
Red-hot chilies to taste (ground or finely slivered)
Vegetables: endive, spring onion, cucumber, etc.—ground red pepper—optional

In a pan on medium heat, mix sugar, nampla, and tamarind liquid until of medium consistency,

Set aside.

In a large pan or wok, lightly brown the garlic and onion in oil.

106

Pad Thai cont...
(Thai Fried Noodle)

Gradually add the meat and shrimp. Put in soy bean sauce. Add tomato, catchup (if used), and rice noodles.

Stir to mix well.

If you use eggs, gather all the mixture aside.

Add a little oil to the pan. Drop the eggs in and stir slightly until cooked.

Roll in all the noodle mixture to cover eggs. Add tofu (if used). Then add ground red pepper (if you like it hot and spicy). Also add half the bean sprouts and the pickled vegetables.

Mix.

Last, pour in the sugar mixture made earlier. Gently stir to blend.

In a serving dish, arrange the noodles in the middle, then top with coarsely ground peanuts.

Arrange selected vegetables around or on the side of the dish.

Garnish with coriander leaves.

Sprinkle lime juice to your taste.

Serves 6-8.

Mèe Grawp
(Special Crispy Noodle)

Mèe Grawp is another of the most well-known of Thai dishes, both in and outside the country. It originated in central Thailand. After proper preparation, this dish will look beautiful. It is composed of long, golden, crispy noodles with a rather pleasant sweet taste and has colorful toppings. This dish is a favorite in Thailand and is chosen for almost every happy ceremony and occasion.

1/2 lb. of rice noodles—about 6 cups

1 cup of cut-up pork

1/2 cup shrimp (peeled, deveined, and cut in half)

1/2 cup chicken (cut up)

1/2 cup yellow bean cake (cut up thinly)

3 eggs—optional

1/2 cup of onion (cut up)

1/4 cup of garlic (cut up)

2 tablespoons tomatoes (cut up)

1 tablespoon black bean sauce

1-2 tablespoons pickled garlic (cut up)

1/2 cup brown sugar (or to taste)

2 tablespoons nampla (fish sauce)

1-2 cups vegetable oil

1 tablespoon lime juice

1 tablespoon vinegar

Vegetables for topping: orange peels, coriander leaves, thinly sliced red peppers, bean sprouts, and ground red pepper.

Dip noodles quickly in boiling water (about 10 seconds).

Drain and dry.

Heat the oil and then fry noodles, a little at a time, until golden brown.

Mèe Grawp cont...
(Special Crispy Noodle)

Separate the noodles nicely. Drain the oil from the noodles.

Fry the pork, chicken, or shrimp about 2 minutes.

Add onion, garlic, bean cake, and stir while cooking for around 5 minutes.

Add eggs, one by one, and scramble them well.

When the mixture starts to dry, add the black bean sauce, pickled garlic, sugar, nampla, vinegar, and tomato. Adjust to taste. Add ground red pepper at this point.

Mix in fried noodles and gently fold in to coat the mixture without breaking the noodles.

You can lift the pan up quickly from the heat to mix and then put it back.

Arrange the noodles in a serving plate and top with orange peel, coriander leaves, bean sprouts, and sliced red peppers.

If you like it sour, add more lime juice to taste.

Serves 8.

Kâo Pad Sapparod
(Fried Rice Pineapple)

This is another one of the beautiful and tasty dishes of the central region.

1 pineapple
6 cups cooked rice
1 cup of chicken or pork (cut up)
1 cup of fresh shrimp (cut up)
2 eggs
2 tablespoons garlic (minced)
1 tablespoon purple onion (minced)
1/3 cup vegetable oil
1-2 tablespoons white soy sauce
1-2 tablespoons nampla (fish sauce)
1 tablespoon sugar
3 stalks coriander leaves (cut up)
Dash of black pepper

Clean the pineapple, then cut in half lengthwise, scoop out the meat, mince, and squeeze out the juice.

Heat the oil in big pan and fry garlic and onion with the meat and shrimp.

When done, add the pineapple, nampla, sugar, and soy sauce.

Make room in the middle to drop in the eggs and scramble them.

Mix the ingredients, then add rice to stir fry and adjust to taste.

Spoon the fried rice into the pineapple lids and garnish with coriander leaves and black pepper.

Serve immediately.

Serves 8-10.

Guay Tiew Reu
(Noodles on a Boat)

Because of its many waterways, Bangkok is called the Venice of the Orient. People who live on the water have food at their front door. The boat noodles have a very special taste and are famous all over Bangkok.

6 cups chicken broth
1 1/4 lbs. flank beef (cut in bite sizes)
1-2 lbs. soup bone and tripe—optional
30 beef balls—optional
1/4 cup light soy sauce
1/4 cup dark soy sauce
1 tablespoon of cinnamon, star anise, and clove (roasted)
4 cloves garlic (2 crushed up and 2 minced and fried in 1/4 cup oil until golden brown)
30 black peppers
10-15 stalks fresh coriander with roots
1-1 1/2 tablespoons rhizome
5-6 tablespoons rice vinegar
5-6 tablespoons nampla (fish sauce)

8 red chili peppers
6 spring onions (minced)
1-2 cups bean sprouts
2 lbs. dried rice noodles
Green vegetables: lettuce, collard green etc.
Dash of sugar

Blend coriander, pepper, rhizome, cinnamon, cloves, star anise, and 2 crushed garlic cloves with both soy sauces. Mix until smooth. In a soup pot, boil chicken broth, beef tripe (if used), and bone. Stir the mixture into the soup and cook on medium-low heat. Wash vegetables and arrange in individual serving bowls. Crush and mix chili peppers with vinegar. Dip noodles into boiling water for 4 or 5 seconds. Drain and toss to coat with garlic oil. Arrange noodles in each bowl. Drop the beef balls into the soup. Boil a few more minutes. Spoon meat and beef balls into the serving bowls. Add vegetables. Top with bean sprouts, nampla, chili vinegar, minced spring onion, and a dash of sugar. Serve with soup. Serves 6.

Kâo Soi
(Northern Style Spicy Noodles)

Kâo Soi was created in the northern part of Thailand. Anyone who has been to Chiengmai (Thailand's second largest city) has probably tried this dish. The pungent taste of lime makes this dish unusual.

2 1/2 lbs. flank beef (cut up)
2 teaspoons curry powder
6 cups coconut milk (set 1/2-1 cup thick cream aside)
5-10 dried red peppers
3-5 tablespoons nampla (fish sauce)
3-4 tablespoons minced garlic (save 1 spoonful for frying)
4-5 tablespoons minced onion (save 1 spoonful for frying)
1 teaspoon ginger (minced)
4-5 teaspoons Five Spices
1-2 tablespoons lemon grass (minced)
1-2 tablespoons galanga
1 tablespoon coriander seed
1 teaspoon salt
8-10 rolls of egg noodles

4 tablespoons coriander leaves (cut up)
2-4 limes (sliced)
2-4 tablespoons dried ground red pepper
6 teaspoons vegetable oil

Marinate meat in curry powder and set aside.

Boil the thick coconut cream and stir well. Set aside.

Put the rest of the coconut milk in a pot. Add meat and cook with low heat until tender.

Blend the following ingredients into a paste: galanga, lemon grass, onion, garlic, coriander seed, dried red pepper, ginger, five spices, and salt.

In big pan, pour a cup of coconut milk from the meat mixture and heat the paste. Gradually add the curry mixture to the meat.

Kâo Soi cont...
(Northern Style Spicy Noodles)

Lower the heat. Add nampla to taste.

Spoon the curry into a serving bowl.

In a pan with oil, mix in 1 teaspoon of onion and 1 teaspoon of garlic (and some ground red pepper if you like it hot).

Cook, stirring until garlic turns golden in color.

Spoon the garlic oil into the bowl.

Dip the noodles into the boiling water quickly (no longer than 5-10 seconds) and mix in with the oil.

Top the noodles with the beef curry.

Top the curry with 1 tablespoon of the cooked coconut cream.

Garnish with coriander leaves.

To serve, arrange the cut-up onions or scallions on the side dish.

For people who prefer a stronger taste, add more dried red pepper and cut-up lime.

Serves 8-10.

Sên Yài Neu Sap
(Ground Beef Noodle)

This dish is quick and easy—suitable for lunch. For people who need more energy, it can be topped with rare fried egg (sunny-side up). It is popular, and one of the most easily obtained dishes in Bangkok and its vicinity.

2 1/2 lbs. wide rice noodle
2 lbs. lean ground beef
8 black peppers (freshly ground)
2 tablespoons Worcestershire sauce
2-3 tablespoons Tang Chai—preserved radish—optional
1 teaspoon curry powder
8 stalks coriander
5-8 cloves garlic (minced)
3 tablespoons vegetable oil
1 tablespoon brown sugar
3-4 tablespoons soy sauce
16 leaves of lettuce
Nampla (to taste)
Thai red-hot pepper sauce—Sriracha (to taste)
Vinegar (to taste)

Blend pepper, Worcestershire sauce, curry powder and coriander. Fold in ground beef to mix well.

Heat pan to fry garlic in oil. Spoon garlic, with some oil, and set aside.

Fry beef in garlic oil. Add a little water, sugar, Tang Chai (if used), half of the soy sauce, and nampla to taste.

Boil noodles quickly (5-7 seconds), then drain and mix well with soy sauce. Set aside.

Arrange lettuce leaves on a serving plate. Top with noodles. Sprinkle the noodles with garlic oil and top with cooked beef and sauce. Then, add a dash of black pepper. Adjust to taste with nampla, sriracha, vinegar, and sugar, as you wish. Serves 8.

Pad Kee Mao
(Drunkard's Noodle)

I must warn you that this recipe is only for a person who really likes it hot and spicy! If you would like to try it, choose the kind of hot peppers wisely (see glossary) and add more sugar to soothe your tongue.

2 1/2 lbs. flank steak, chicken breast, lean pork, or shrimp (cut up bite-size)
2 1/2 lbs. dried rice noodle (soaked in warm water for 5-10 minutes)
5-6 cloves garlic
10-15 whole black peppers
10-15 coriander roots or seed
5-7 green, red, and yellow chili peppers
1/2 cup purple onion (sliced)
3 tablespoons nampla (or to taste)
1-2 tablespoons brown sugar
1-2 tablespoons rice vinegar
1/2 cup Italian tomatoes
2-3 tablespoons vegetable oil to fry

1/2 cup of morning glory or spinach
1/2 cup basil or mint
5-6 peppercorns—optional
Sriracha Sauce

Blend garlic, pepper, coriander roots, and hot chili peppers.

In a wok or big frying pan, heat oil to fry the mixture. Add meat pieces and stir fry quickly, then add the onion.

Continue to stir fry well (about 30 seconds). Add nampla, sugar, vinegar, tomatoes, and noodles—mixing well. Add morning glory or spinach, basil, or mint, and peppercorns. Stir quickly to mix, then remove immediately.

Serve hot, with Sriracha sauce, if you prefer.

Serves 8-10.

Kâo Man
(Coconut Steamed Rice)

central Thai version of rice is created to serve with Sôm Tum, hot curries (chicken or beef), and other chicken dishes, instead of the sticky rice served by the northeastern Thais.

3 cups of long-grain rice (washed)
3 1/2 cups thin coconut milk or low fat milk
2-3 teaspoons salt
2 teaspoons sugar

Bring coconut milk and rice to a boil.

Add salt and sugar to the pot, then reduce heat to low and simmer with lid on until rice absorbs all the milk.

Open to check after 15-18 minutes.

Stir and fluff it. Serves 6-8.

Kâo Kari
(Rice Curry)

2 cups long-grain rice (washed)

3 cups water or stock

2-3 tablespoons vegetable oil

1 tablespoon light soy sauce

1 teaspoon ginger (minced)

1 teaspoon curry powder

2 teaspoons salt

1 teaspoon parsley or basil

1/2 teaspoon garlic powder or fresh garlic (minced)

1/2 teaspoon cumin

1/2 teaspoon cardamom

1/4-1/2 teaspoon ground dried red pepper

1/2 cup mushrooms—preferably wood fungus (cut up)

Heat oil to high and coat rice well.

Add water or stock to boil rice for 2 minutes.

Stir in soy, ginger, curry powder, salt, parsley, (or basil), garlic, cumin, cardamom, pepper, and mushrooms and simmer with the lid on for 20 minutes.

Do not stir again.

Remove from heat and let set for 10 minutes before serving.

Serves 4-6.

117

Kâo Taud
(Spicy Rice Balls)

I include this dish because it is my father's favorite kind of rice. It is a food from the northern part of Thailand. When served with Nam Sod, it can be a satisfying lunch.

5 cups cooked rice (long grained)
1 cup lean ground pork
5 dried red-hot peppers (soaked in water and deseeded)
2 teaspoons coriander roots or seed
1 teaspoon shrimp paste—optional
4 teaspoons purple onion or shallots (minced)
2-3 teaspoons garlic (minced)
2-3 tablespoons nampla (fish sauce)
Dash of sugar
1/2 cup of coconut milk
1/2 cup egg white (beat well)
1 1/2 cups mixture of rice or wheat flour or corn flour
Vegetable oil to fry
Blend red peppers, coriander roots, shrimp paste, onion, and garlic.

Roll in ground pork with nampla, a dash of sugar, and cooked rice.

Then make 2" x 2" rice balls and set aside.

Mix coconut milk, egg whites.

Dip rice balls in the coconut mixture, roll in the flour mixture to coat, then fry in medium hot oil (semi-deep fry).

Drain the balls and serve hot with Nam Sod (see Appetizers).

Serves 12.

Kâo Pad Thai Tae
(Classical Thai Fried Rice)

Originally, fried rice was created because the housewives did not want to throw away left-over rice or meats. Asian people tend to cook more than enough food—especially rice. Any house party that does not have enough food for the guests suffers endless shame (loosing face) and endless gossip. The next day, in trying to conserve, one lady of the house found a way to create a new dish.

8 cups cooked jasmine rice or long-grain rice
1/2 cup each of pork, shrimp or chicken (cut into bite-sizes)
1/2 cup vegetable oil
1-2 tablespoons garlic (minced)
2-3 eggs (beaten)
3 tablespoons nampla (or to taste)
2 tablespoons sugar (or to taste)
4 tablespoons Catchup
5-7 stalks of coriander (for garnish)
5 red peppers (julienne)
1-2 limes (sliced)
Dash of pepper
1-2 cucumbers (partly peeled and sliced thinly)
8 stalks green onions (cut in half)
Sriracha sauce

Heat oil to fry garlic until light gold. Add pork, shrimp, or chicken. Stir fry for 2-3 minutes. When the meat is cooked, gradually roll in rice and stir to mix well. Make room in the middle of the pan and break eggs into the space and scramble while adding nampla and sugar, then the catchup. Stir quickly to mix well. Use rather high heat. Remove the pan and spoon the rice into a serving bowl. Add a dash of pepper and garnish with red pepper, coriander leaves, cucumber. Add green onion, and lime on the side.

Serve hot with 1 tablespoon Sriracha sauce or nampla mixed with 1 tablespoon of lime juice and red pepper (if you like it hot). This could be served as a main lunch dish. Serves 8.

Thai Desserts

Thai desserts are composed of varieties of tropical fruits, such as banana, mango, coconut, jackfruit, longan, and even tamarind. The flours mostly used include: rice flour and sweet-rice flour. Sticky rice is as popular for Thai dessert as coconut milk. Mung bean and sweet potato are used as often as taro, cassava, and tapioca pearls. The extracts commonly used are jasmine, vanilla, bandan, and rose extract. To make it look good, food colors may also be added.

The Thai art of carving fruits and creating desserts to help beautify any ceremony goes a long way back in history. Names, appearances, tastes, and ingredients are often described in poems and classical literature. Desserts are chosen in the same manner as main courses to be served on festive occasions. Believe it or not, nobody serves "baa bin" at any ceremony or happy party. This delicious and popular dessert is sold at most street-corner stands and in front of most movie theaters.

Gluey Buad Chee
(Ordained Banana)

Another creative way to make the good old banana more interesting is to "ordain" her. This dessert turns out to be delightful. You can decide if the name fits its appearance or not.

8 bananas (cut length-wise into halves)
1 drop of jasmine or rose extract
2 1/2 cups medium-thin coconut milk
1/2 cup brown sugar
1/4 teaspoon salt
1/3 cup of ground roasted peanuts
1-2 tablespoons roasted sesame seeds (for garnish)
Steam bananas with peels on until medium rare.

Then cut into half again, peel off, and drop into the pot with coconut milk, a drop of jasmine or rose extract, sugar, and salt.

Let it boil for 3-5 minutes before removing from heat.

Spoon the bananas into an individual serving bowl and top with sesame seeds and peanuts.

Serve hot.

Serves 12.

Kanom Maw Gang
(Taro or Mung Bean Custard)

This is one of the classic desserts of the central region. It is served at many parties and ceremonies. You can find it not only in restaurants (big or small) but also at almost every street-corner stand, especially in front of the movie theaters at all times of the day or night.

2 cups cooked mashed taro or mung bean

4 eggs (beaten)

2 tablespoons rice flour

1/4 teaspoon salt

3/4 cup brown sugar

2 tablespoons white sugar

2 cups coconut milk

3/4 teaspoon vanilla extract

1/2 cup onion (thinly sliced and sautéed in oil and drained)

Soak beans in warm water for 15-30 minutes, then drain. Steam beans or taro (if used) on medium heat for about 30 minutes.

Blend beans, or taro, in food processor to make a coarse paste.

Beat eggs well, then add flour, salt, sugar, coconut milk, and bean or taro paste. Stir in vanilla extract. Stir over low heat until thick.

Warm 13" x 9" shallow baking pan first. Then, grease and pour custard into the pan. Bake in 350°F. for about 30 minutes, then turn up the oven to broil for 2-3 minutes to make the top crispy and golden brown.

Remove and sprinkle fried onion slices over the custard. Let cool and cut.

Serves 12-16.

Sarim
(Vishnu in Milky Sea)

For hot and humid days in Thailand, Sarim is the best of many ice-cold desserts (at least for me). Isn't the translation descriptive enough for your imagination?

1/2 cup mung bean flour (sarim flour can be found in Thai groceries)
2-3 cups of water
Few drops of jasmine or rose extract
Green and red food coloring
1/2 cup thick coconut milk
1 1/2 cups sugar
1 1/2 cups water
dash of salt
Crushed ice

Heat pot with 2 cups of water, a drop of extract, and flour. Stir over low heat until flour is cooked and clear and does not drip from spoon.

Divide the flour into two parts.

Color one part pale green and the other pink. In ricer, push each color of flour mixture into bowls of very cold water.

When the noodle-like dessert becomes firm, drain and chill.

Boil 1 1/2 cups of sugar and 1 1/2 cups of water with 1 drop of extract.

Remove, and mix in coconut milk and a dash of salt and chill.

To serve, spoon the dessert, the same or both colors, depending on your taste, into individual cups.

Pour in the coconut mixture and top with crushed ice.

Serve 4-6.

124

Tago
(Cassava or Longan Pudding)

1 3/4 lbs. cassava or longan
3 1/2 cups water
3 cups brown sugar
3-4 cups coconut milk
1/2 teaspoon white sugar
1-1 1/2 teaspoons salt
2 tablespoons rice flour
4 tablespoons cassava flour or corn flour
2 drops jasmine extract

Blend cassava, brown sugar, and water.

Spoon into half of the individual cups and steam until done.

Remove and set aside.

If you use longan, cook the mixture of sugar, water, and 6 tablespoons of both flours until thick, then add the longan (fresh, if possible) then set aside.

Topping for cassava pudding:

Mix coconut milk, white sugar, salt, 6 tablespoons of both flours, and 2 drops of extract.

Stir mixture in a sauce pan over low heat until done and top the cassava cups to serve.

Topping for longan pudding:

Mix coconut milk, white sugar, salt, and the jasmine extract. Cook and top the longan cups.

Serves 16.

125

Saku Maprao Oan
(Tapioca Coconut Pudding)

A simple and delicious dessert.

3/4-1 cup pearl tapioca
2-3 cups water
2 drops jasmine or rose extract
1/4-1/2 teaspoon salt
1/2 cup sugar
6 oz young coconut meat (fresh, canned, or dried)
1/2 cup coconut cream

Boil water and add the extract, tapioca, and salt.

Stir until cooked—10-15 minutes.

Add sugar and coconut meat. Add a dash of salt into the coconut cream and warm up.

Top each serving bowl with a spoonful of the cream before serving.

Serves 8.

126

Sankaya Fakthong
(Pumpkin Flan)

This dessert is especially healthy.

1 medium pumpkin or acorn squash
3 eggs (beaten)
1/2 cup brown sugar
1 1/2 cup coconut milk
1/2 teaspoon vanilla or 1/4 bandan—Bai Teoy—extract
Dash of salt

Wash pumpkin and cut off the top.

Remove seeds and spongy tissue to make it smooth.

Mix the coconut milk with eggs, sugar, extract, and a dash of salt.

Stir well, then pour the custard into the pumpkin and place the pumpkin in a heat proof bowl.

Steam the topless pumpkin in boiling water for about 45 minutes.

Cool and cut 10-12 wedges.

Remove the skin, serve both pumpkin and custard.

Serves 10-12.

Tuptim Grawp
(Crispy Ruby)

During midsummer, this dessert really hits the spot, not just because of its refreshing taste, but also because of its tantalizingly beautiful look.

2 cups diced water chestnut, jicama or pear
3/4 cup water with few drops of red food color
3/4 cup cornstarch
1 1/2 cups medium-thick coconut milk
1 drop jasmine extract
1 cup white sugar
1 cup of water
Crushed ice
Dash of salt

Make the syrup by boiling one cup of water with jasmine extract and one cup of sugar.

Boil coconut milk with a dash of salt. Set aside.

Soak water chestnut pieces in colored water for few minutes. Spoon them out, drain, and coat them in cornstarch.

In a pot of boiling water, gradually drop them in to cook— 3 minutes.

Spoon the cooked chestnut pieces out and drop them in ice cold water, drain, and set aside.

Arrange chestnuts in an individual serving bowl. Top with syrup, coconut milk, and crushed ice.

Serves 6-8.

Plagrim Peug
(Taro Delight)

1 1/2 cups cooked taro (mashed)
2 1/2 cups sweet-rice flour
10 tablespoons hot water
3 1/2 cups coconut milk
1 cup brown sugar
3 tablespoons white sugar (or less)
1 teaspoon salt

Pour hot water into sweet-rice flour and stir quickly. Mix in taro.

Flatten the mixture and cut into 2" slices.

Boil coconut milk, 2 kinds of sugar, and salt, then drop in the taro slices.

When done, they pop up. Serve in individual bowls.

Serves 10.

Kanom Talai
(Colorful Sesame Balls)

...sert is colorful. Even though the procedure is a little complicated, you will agree that success makes it worthwhile.

3 cups rice flour
1/2 cup and 3 tablespoons toasted sesame seeds
3/4 teaspoon salt
1/4 teaspoon vanilla or 1 drop of jasmine extract
7 1/2 cups water
1/2 cup brown sugar
1/2 cup white sugar
1/2 cup coarsely ground peanuts
1/2 cup coconut flakes
green and red food colors

Mix flour, 3 tablespoons sesame seeds, and 1/4 teaspoon salt. Divide the mixture into 3 parts. Set aside.

Mix 1 1/2 cups water with vanilla or jasmine extract and divide water into 3 equal portions. Add food colors to 2 portions (one color each) and leave one portion without color.

Add each part of the dough to each portion of water and knead for 5 minutes. Form small balls of dough.

Mix 1/2 cup of brown sugar, peanuts, and coconut flakes well, then insert the mixture into every ball (about 1/3 teaspoon each).

Boil 6 cups water and 1/2 teaspoon salt. Drop flour balls gradually. When all the balls float, drain and let cool.

Mix coconut flakes, sesame seeds, and half cup of each sugar. Roll the colorful balls in the mixture and arrange on a serving plate. Serves 12.

Kâo Neo Piak Lumyài
(Rice Longan)

2 cups sweet rice (washed well)
5 cups water with a few drops of rose extract
25 longans (fresh or canned)
1 1/4 lbs. white sugar
1 cup thick coconut milk
1/3 teaspoon salt

Cook sweet rice in boiling water.

Add longan and sugar.

Remove from heat.

Warm coconut milk and salt to top each bowl of pudding.

Serves 8-10.

Buo Lawy
(Floating Lily Buds)

This sweet is as fun to make as it is to eat. It is one of the most popular Thai desserts.

1 cup cassava flour or tapioca flour
3 cups sweet-rice flour
4 cups thin and 1 cup thick coconut milk
1 cup white and 1/2 cup brown sugar
1 teaspoon salt
1-2 drops of Jasmine extract

Knead flour with water (about 10 tablespoons) and make small balls.

Cover with a thin cloth. Let stand for 10 minutes.

Boil water and drop flour balls in.

When they all float, drain and pour into cool water.

Mix sugar, half teaspoon salt, and thin coconut milk.

Add 1 drop of Jasmine extract and bring to boil.

Drain the flour balls from water and pour into the pot and turn the heat down to simmer.

Add a dash of salt to the thick coconut milk and then warm it.

Before serving, top individual cup with thick coconut milk to taste, but do not stir.

Serves 14-16.

Taro Buo Lawy
(Floating Taro Balls)

2 1/2 cups sweet-rice flour
1 1/2 cups taro (cooked and mashed)
10 tablespoons water
3 1/2 cups medium-thick coconut milk
1 cup brown sugar
3 tablespoons white sugar
1 teaspoons salt

Knead flour, taro, and water and form into small balls.

Mix coconut milk and both kinds of sugar and salt.

Cook on low heat.

Drop the flour balls into the pot.

When the balls pop up, remove and serve in a small bowl.

Serves 14.

Saku Tang Thai
(Tapioca Pearl with Cantaloupe)

1 cup tapioca pearl
5 cups water
1-2 drops of Jasmine extract
1/2 teaspoon salt
1/2 cup sugar
1 cup medium-thick coconut milk
1 ripened cantaloupe (spooned out or cut into small chunks)

Boil water. Add extract, tapioca, and salt, stir occasionally until cooked (about 5-10 minutes).

Add sugar and coconut milk.

Remove from heat.

Drop in cantaloupe chunks, mix, and serve in individual bowls. Serves 14.

134

Krong Krang Gati
(Shells with Coconut Milk)

3 cups rice flour

3 cups water

2 tablespoons tapioca or cassava flour

4 cups medium-thin and 1 cup thick coconut milk

1/4 cup white sugar

1 tablespoon salt

1/4 cup white sesame seeds (browned)

In a pan, combine water, rice flour, and one tablespoon tapioca flour, then stir while cooking on low.

When the mixture comes off the pan easily, remove from heat and let stand to cool.

At the kneading board, coat the cooked flour in one tablespoon tapioca flour, knead, and form small balls.

Use fork to make the flour balls into small shells.

In a pot, boil 4 cups of medium thin coconut milk with salt and sugar. Drop in the flour shells to cook.

When they are transparent in color, remove from heat.

Warm the thick coconut milk with dash of salt.

To serve, spoon the shells and coconut milk into individual bowls.

Top with thick coconut milk, and sprinkle with the sesame seeds.

Serves 4-6.

Kanoon Cake
(Jackfruit Cake)

2 cups cake flour
2 teaspoons baking powder
1/2 teaspoon salt
1 cup butter
1 1/4 cups sugar
3 eggs
1/4 cup milk
1 1/2 teaspoons vanilla extract
1 1/2 cups fresh jackfruit or 1 can drained (cut up)
1/4 cup crushed peanuts

Mix baking powder, flour, and salt and set aside.

Beat butter.

Gradually mix in sugar, until light, then blend in eggs—one by one.

Mix in flour, milk, vanilla extract. Blend well. Add jackfruit last.

In a buttered pan, pour in the cake mixture up to 3/4 of the pan.

Sprinkle with peanuts and bake in 350°F. for about 30-40 minutes.

Serves 16.

Kanom Gluey
(Banana Delight)

As I have mentioned before, the banana is so abundant in Thailand, the word "gluey" (banana) became an idiom and means "easy." Kanom gluey is the dessert that fits its name.

1 1/2 cups mashed banana
1/2 cup rice flour
1/4 cup corn or tapioca starch
1/2 cup brown sugar
2 tablespoons white sugar
1/2 cup coconut milk
1/4 cup fresh coconut meat or unsweetened dried coconut flakes (grated)
1/4 teaspoon salt

Mix banana, rice flour, and tapioca starch with both kinds of sugar.

Blend the mixture with coconut milk until smooth.

Mix coconut flake with salt and set aside.

Fill small cups with the mixture and top with the coconut flakes.

Steam until done—20-30 minutes.

Serves 8.

137

Kanom Kài Nok
(Bird Egg Dessert)

1/2 cup of medium-thick coconut milk
1 egg—optional
1 1/4 lbs. sweet potatoes (cooked and mashed)
3/4 cup white sugar
1/2 teaspoon salt
1 cup cassava flour
1/4 cup wheat flour
2-3 tablespoons water
Vegetable oil

Heat vegetable oil and fry the flour balls on low heat.

When they become light brown and crispy, remove from heat and drain oil.

Warm coconut milk, with a dash of salt, to top each individual serving plate.

Serves 14-16.

Steam sweet potatoes. Peel and mash them—measuring about 2 1/2 cups.

Mix the mashed potatoes with sugar, salt, flour, water, and egg (if used) and knead until smooth.

Make small balls out of the flour mixture and set aside.

Kâo Niew Ping
(Sweet Rice & Banana)

This is another original idea to hide a banana from sight as a surprise! It is rather ironic that we have to use its leaves to hide its own fruit. Who would suspect we could be that smart?

4 cups sweet rice (soaked in water for 4 hrs., or in very warm water for 20 minutes, and drained)
2 1/2 cups medium-thin coconut milk
1 1/2 tablespoons salt
4 tablespoons white sugar
4 ripened bananas (cut into 16 pieces)
Foil to wrap (in place of banana leaves)
1 cup unsweetened grated or shredded coconut

In a deep pan, on medium heat, mix sweet rice, coconut milk, salt and sugar. Stir occasionally, until the water evaporates.

Cut foil into 7" pieces. Wrap sweet rice around banana pieces and seal tightly.

Bake on low heat until rice turns golden brown—or you can use the steaming method.

Open the foil and top the cooked sweet rice with shredded coconut.

Cut into bite-sizes before serving.

Serves 16.

Baa Bin
(Crazy Cassava)

Just because "baa bin" means raving mad, and nobody picks this dessert to serve at a party, does not mean that it does not taste good. After trying it, you will feel sorry for its name.

2 cups cassava (shredded)
3 cups shredded coconut (unsweetened)
1 1/2 cups white sugar
1 teaspoon salt
1/2 teaspoon vanilla extract

Mix the ingredients well, pour into buttered pan.

Bake in 400°F. until golden brown.

Cut into square pieces.

Serves 12-16.

Mango Ice Cream

3 large ripened mangoes (peeled and chopped)
1/2 teaspoon salt
1 cup white sugar
1 cup whipping cream
1 cup thick coconut milk
2-3 tablespoons fresh orange juice

In a blender, mix salt, sugar, and mango, gradually mixing in whip cream, coconut milk, and orange juice, until smooth.

Pour the mixture in a tray and place in the freezer until almost frozen.

Scrap the mixture into the blender and blend in low cycle.

Put the blended ice cream into the freezer again.

Serve after dinner with cake or on top mango.

Serves 8-10.

Sankaya Kanoon
(Jackfruit Flan)

1 cup brown sugar
1 cup egg white or whole egg (well beaten)
3/4-1 cup medium-thick coconut milk
1/2 teaspoon vanilla or one drop of jasmine extract
About 1/2 teaspoon salt
1 1/2 cups fresh jackfruit or one 15 oz. can (sliced)
1/2 cup almond slivers

Mix sugar and egg in low cycle for ten minutes while gradually folding in coconut milk, extract, and salt. Stir well.

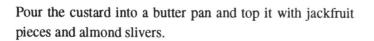

Pour the custard into a butter pan and top it with jackfruit
pieces and almond slivers.

Steam in boiling water for 15-20 minutes or until done.

Cool and cut to serve. Serves 12.

Loy Kaow
(Floating Crystals)

6 cups water
4-5 cups sugar
1-2 drops jasmine extract
2-3 teaspoons salt
1 lime (cut into 4-5 slices)
A variety of preferred fruits: Rambutan, longan, pineapple, mango, grape, orange, grapefruit, cantaloupe etc. (cut up the way you like)

Boil water with extract, adding sugar, salt, and lime last— for three minutes.

Let cool.

In serving cup, arrange fruit pieces.

Top with crushed ice and pour syrup over.

Serves 6-8.

143

Kâo Neiw Mamuong
(Sweet Rice & Mango)

One of the best things that comes with summer in tropical countries, especially Thailand, is Kâo Neiw Mamuong. The mamuong (mango) that is best for this special kind of prepared rice is called "ogrong," the sweetest and most delicious of the species.

If ogrong is not available, choose the very ripest and biggest mango you can find.

2 cups long-grained sweet rice (steamed)
1 1/2 cups thick coconut milk
1-2 tablespoons sugar (or to taste)
1/4-1/2 teaspoon salt
5-6 ripe mangoes
2 tablespoons coconut cream
4 tablespoons roasted mung beans

In a mixing bowl, mix warm, steamed, sweet rice with coconut milk, sugar, and salt. Cover the bowl with foil for at least 30 minutes.

Mix coconut cream with sugar and dash of salt—optional.

To serve, arrange rice in the middle of a serving plate. Peel mango (half at a time) and chop into about 1 1/2" pieces. Lay them around the rice.

You can also cut mango in half with the skin on and spoon the meat off—like melon.

Top the rice with mixed coconut cream and sprinkle with roasted mung beans.

Serves 4-6.

Med Kanoon
(Mock Kanoon Seed)

Several kinds of Thai desserts are made from egg yolk and are very sweet and rich. This one is the least sweet. It is made mostly from mung beans or taro or potato, not just the egg yolk with heavy syrup. Its shape is supposed to look like the seed of a kanoon (jackfruit). Med Kanoon is not only delicious in taste, but also fun to make.

2 1/2 cups of mung bean, taro, or potato (boiled, peeled and mashed finely)
1 1/2 cups thick coconut milk
1 1/4 cups brown sugar
3/4 cup of unsweetened coconut (grated)
2 cups of water mixed with 1 drop of jasmine extract
2 cups of granulated sugar
7 egg yolks (beaten well)

Mix mashed mung bean (or taro, or potato), with coconut milk, brown sugar, and grated coconut to cook in a deep pan. Stir the mixture continuously until it becomes thick—like bread dough. Remove from heat, when it is cool. Roll the dough into small balls the size of your thumb.

Boil 2 cups of jasmine water and 2 cups of granulated sugar. Keep stirring until the syrup sticks to the spoon. Remove and set aside to cool.

Dip the small mung bean balls into the beaten egg yolk, and drop them into the pan full of syrup. Then cook the syrup, with those balls, on low heat. When the egg around the Med Kanoon balls is cooked, spoon them up.

Arrange 3-4 balls in an individual plate.

Serve cold.

Serve 14.

Naree Long Sòng
(Lady Bathing)

Wait until you see this dish's appearance. You will agree that the person who named it has a mischievous mind.

1 cup thick and 3 cups medium-thin coconut milk
1-1 1/2 cups sugar
2/3 teaspoon salt
2 good looking sweet potatoes (peel and dice)
5 half-ripened bananas (peel and slice 1/2" thick)
1 cup cooked small red beans
Dash of salt

Mix 3 cups medium-thin coconut milk with sugar and salt, then cook over medium heat while stirring.

When the coconut milk is boiling, drop in potato cubes and banana slices. Cover the pot. Open to stir occasionally.

When both banana and potato are done, add the beans and stir. Let boil a few more minutes.

Remove and serve in individual bowl.

Top with thick coconut milk mixed with a dash of salt.

Serves 10.

146

Cake Makham
(Tamarind Cake)

This cake has an unusually pleasant mixture of tastes (tart, sweet, and nutty) from fruits and nuts. You can serve with or without frosting. Sweet frosting goes well with it.

1 3/4 cups of cake flour
1 teaspoon of baking soda
1/2 teaspoon baking powder
1 teaspoon of cinnamon
1/4 teaspoon of salt
1/2 teaspoon clove s (ground)
3/4 cup vegetable oil
1 cup of sugar
1 egg (well beaten)
1 cup of tamarind liquid
1 cup of yellow raisins
1 cup ground dried roasted peanuts (unsalted)

Make tamarind liquid by boiling 1/4 cup of water. Drop about 2" x 2" pieces of tamarind paste to dissolve, then squeeze the thick liquid through fine sieve. Dilute the liquid with water to make 1 cup.

Mix and sift flour, baking soda, baking powder, cinnamon, clove, and salt, well. Set aside.

Beat oil with sugar—gradually. Blend in egg and continue to beat until light. Gradually stir in flour and tamarind liquid. Mix in raisins and peanuts.

Pour the cake into a greased pan and bake in 350° F. oven for about 45-55 minutes.

Cut and serve.

Serve 12-16.

Glossary

Glossary

Aubergine (Eggplant)—The most popular kind of eggplant used in Thai cooking is the pea aubergine—the size of a pea. It can be found in almost all Asian food stores. The white, lime green, or blackish-purple aubergine may be substituted.

Banana Leaves—Banana is an indispensable plant in most tropical countries. Its leaf is used to wrap, store, and serve food. Food can be cooked, steamed, and grilled in banana leaf to attain special flavor and color. It is also used in arts and crafts in Thai's everyday life. Once refrigerated, it can be kept for months. If banana leaf is unavailable, foil can be substituted, though this may not result in food having the same flavor.

Basil (Holy or Sweet)—Known as "horapa" in Thai. Horapa has a darker leaf than the European basil, but the two can be substituted. It normally has a purple stem and a strong, cinnamon-like flavor. Fresh basil is available in most oriental grocery stores. It is also very easy to grow outdoors in summer, or all year by an indoor window. You can substitute dried leaves for fresh basil by soaking in water and draining before using. Just use twice the amount of fresh basil called for in the recipe.

Bean Sauces, Cakes, or Paste (Black, Red, Yellow)—Pungent and salty sauces are made from preserved soy beans, garlic, water, salt, sugar, rice wine, and soy bean oil. They come in bottles, cans, or jars found in most Asian grocery. They should be refrigerated after opening, but can be kept up to six months.

Bean Sprouts—Fresh bean sprouts can be home grown by sprinkling green mung beans, that have first been soaked in water overnight, on several layers of wet tissue papers. Place the paper in a plastic bucket and then put it in a warm spot (e.g., under the kitchen sink). Both fresh bean sprouts and mung beans are easily available in Asian food stores,

150

Glossary

heath food stores, or supermarkets. They can be stored in a refrigerator in a tightly sealed plastic bag, or in water that is changed daily, for a week or longer.

Bean Threads (Cellophane Noodles)—Sometimes called transparent noodles, they are very fine noodles made from mung bean flour. They come in a small packet and have to be soaked in warm water before using or, in some recipes, they can be deep-fried right from the packets.

Bitter Melon (Balsam Pear or Balsam Apple)—Mara (Thai name) is a green, cucumber-shaped, tropical melon, with ridges and knobs around the skin. Before cooking, it must be cut in half and the seeds scooped out, then soaked (10 minutes) or boiled (2-3 minutes) in salty water, drained and dried. This kind of melon is good for making soup or curry, or just to stir-fry with shrimp, meat or eggs.

Cardamom—This is one of the most essential ingredients in Thai cooking. A member of the ginger family, varieties of cardamom seed pods come in brown or pale green colors. They can be used whole, bruised, or ground. For best results, roast the cardamom before using (on high in microwave for 1 minute). To make ground cardamom, crack open and grind just before using to obtain full flavor. Cardamom is used only in small amounts for a special flavor. Whole or ground cardamom is available in most grocery stores and health food stores.

Cassava, Tapioca, and Tapioca Pearl—This is a long potato-like root with a hard bark. When it comes in flaky or pearly form, it is called tapioca. The young root can be peeled and cooked (whole, cut, or grated) into a variety of delicious desserts. Tapioca pearls and flour can also be found in Asian groceries.

Glossary

Chili—Thai hot chilies come in many sizes and colors and should be handled with extreme caution. The smallest in size (bird's eye or bird pepper) is the hottest. It is called "prík kee nùu" and comes in red and green. The bigger size, called "prík chee faa", can be yellow in color and is milder than prík kee nùu. All sizes of peppers can be dried and ground into powder. Mexican finger peppers can be used as a substitute to obtain a similar flavor and color, but with a milder taste.

Coconut & Coconut Milk—Young (green) coconut, with its soft white flesh and refreshing juice, is for drinking and some dishes or desserts only. The creamy and rich liquid extract is made from the grated meat of the fresh mature coconut. This milk is indispensable in Thai cooking and curries. These are three methods to obtain coconut milk:

1) From can: The canned coconut milk is available in most Asian groceries. For thick milk, use without diluting with water. For medium milk, mix with one-half can of water and for thin milk, mix in an equal amount of water. For recipes that call for coconut cream, just spoon the cream from the top of the can.

2) Fresh milk: You can make at home by baking a fresh, mature coconut in 400° F. for 15 minutes. Hammer it open (in a plastic bag so that you can preserve the water for drinking, if you like). Then separate the meat from the husk, peel off the brown skin and grate the meat with a food processor. Blend one cup of grated meat with one cup of very warm water for thick milk. Strain the mixture through a fine strainer into a bowl (press hard with wooden spoon). For the medium milk, repeat the process for a second time. The third time, you will get thin milk.

3) From unsweetened (desiccated) shredded coconut flakes (if nothing else is available): Use one cup of hot water and one cup of flakes. Blend on high speed for one minute, strain (as in the second method) and use. The result is thick coconut milk. For medium coconut milk, repeat the extraction process, using the same amount of water and the same

Glossary

coconut flakes used to make the thick milk. For thin coconut milk, repeat the extraction process a third time. Coconut milk can be kept in the freezer for a long period of time.

Coriander (Cilantro)—Thai food will not be authentic without coriander. The closest substitute for fresh coriander leaves is coriander seed (bottled or packaged). All parts of the plant are used. Roots (cleaned) are used in some Thai curry pastes (the base of the stem can be added if there is not enough root). Leaves are used whole or are chopped into seasoning mixtures. Fresh coriander or cilantro (Mexican name) is available in most Asian grocery stores and in some supermarkets. Coriander seeds have a milder, lemon-like flavor, and are very frequently used ground up in curry pastes, mixtures for marinating, and in soups. Whole coriander seeds look like white peppercorns. It is very easy to grow coriander. Just soak the seeds in water over night and sprinkle with soil and water every day. Grow in the sun or indoors near a window. To use, just pull up, with roots attached, when they are 5-6 inches tall. Do not let them go to seed. Coriander can be stored in the refrigerator (in a bottle with water, including roots), for weeks.

Cumin (Yira)—The Thai name is yira. Like coriander, it is an essential ingredient in Thai cuisine. It is mostly used in curry and in marinades. For best results in terms of aroma, it should be roasted before using (in a microwave on high for about 1 minute). Cumin, whole or ground seeds, is available in almost all supermarkets and Asian grocery stores.

Dried Shrimp (Kung Hang)—Kung hang (Thai name), is very often used in salads, curries, and soups. It comes both whole (various sizes) or ground (which may or may not be mixed with chili powder). Most oriental food stores carry dried shrimp.

Glossary

Galanga (Laos or Kha)—Thais call it kha. It is a member of ginger family, and has an orange-red hue. If used fresh, it can add a special aromatic flavor to a dish. Outside Southeast Asia, dried galanga is available, both sliced and ground, in oriental markets. Dried sliced pieces should be soaked in warm water before using.

Garlic, Garlic Oil & Pickled Garlic—Like Italian cuisine, Thai cooking uses lots of garlic. Normally Thai or Asian garlic comes in a much smaller size than in America. Usually, I crush garlic lightly and the peel comes right off. Then I mince it finely before using. To make garlic oil, just deep fry the minced garlic, until a light golden color, on medium heat (do not over cook), then spoon all garlic and oil into a bottle. It lasts indefinitely in the refrigerator. It can be used to garnish or give flavor to the dishes and also used with a stir-fried recipe that calls for minced garlic (if you are pressed for time).

To make pickled garlic, dissolve 2 tablespoons sugar and 2 tablespoons salt and 3/4 pint white vinegar (about 1 2/3 cups). Boil well. When cool, pour over the cloves of 2 garlic bulbs (cleaned and partly peeled). Then seal in a preserve jar for 7-10 days. For recipes that call for pickled garlic, peel and use.

Ginger or Pickled Ginger—It is a sandy or reddish-brown aromatic tropical plant. This pungent plant is used as a spice, in medicine, and for perfumes. Thais use ginger in many dishes, including sweets and ice cream. Pickling ginger is one way to store it. To pickle ginger, use 2 1/2 lbs. peeled ginger with 3 cups of nampla, 3 cups of brown sugar, and 3 cups of rice vinegar. Boil and let cool. Score the ginger root very finely and put it into this mixture, seal and refrigerate. Another way to store ginger is to peel the roots, cut and pack the ginger chunks in a bottle, cover them with dry sherry, seal and refrigerate. Fresh ginger is preferable, though powder can also be used if necessary.

Glossary

Jack Fruit—This is a delicious and popular tropical fruit, with rough yellow-green skin and golden colored flesh. Thais use both the flesh and seeds to make many hot and cold desserts. Canned jack fruit from several countries in Southeast Asia is available in most Asian groceries.

Kaffir Lime Leaves (Citrus Leaves from the Magrut plant)—Thais call it magrut. The magrut plant has beautiful shiny green leaves and can be easily grown in full sun or indoors near a window. This is the variety of citrus for which the juice, rind, and leaves are used frequently in Thai cooking, especially in curries and hot pastes. The skin is minced and blended in curry paste and the juice is used in salad dressings and sauces. The leaves are slivered to garnish, or used whole in soup or curry. Normally, whole leaves should be removed from the dish before serving (especially to non-Thais!) just like bay leaves. Dried kaffir lime peel and leaves from Thailand can be found in all Thai or Asian markets.

Lemon Grass—A tropical plant with aromatic citrus flavor. It has a white bulbous base and grass-like leaves, but we use only the whitest core (3" - 4") and discard the sharp, green leaves. If the recipe calls for the stalk, pound it before using and remove it from the dish before serving—specially in soup. If it calls for minced bulb, just slice very thinly before adding (to be blended into a paste etc.). Lemon grass is available in most oriental markets (fresh or dried). You can store it in a bottle of water (with roots), and refrigerate. It will keep for weeks and grow roots. Cut the roots off before using. You can grow lemon grass by planting the stalk outdoors or in a pot near an indoor window. It grows easily and rapidly in full sun.

Lime & Lime Juice—Instead of lemons, Thais use the lime and lime juice in cooking for more pungent flavor. Lime is another of the essential ingredients in Thai cuisine. Thais put lime juice in fried eggs so that they will stay fluffy longer. It is also used in salad dressings and in most Thai mixed sauces. Thais also drink limeade (with a dash of salt!) instead of lemonade.

Glossary

Mace & Nutmeg—These spices are often used in Thai curry paste and come in both whole or ground form. Sometimes they are used to tone down a fishy smell and are mostly used in the ground form.

Mung Bean Flour and Noodles—Mung beans are small and greenish-yellow. Thais use the beans inside the husks in desserts, such as Kanom Maw Gang. Mung bean flour is used to make fine transparent noodles (called woon sên). Mung bean vermicelli, also called cellophane noodles, are sold in packets in most Asian groceries.

Nampla (Fish Sauce)—Nampla is among the most basic of ingredients in Thai and most other Southeast Asian cuisines. Every country has its own version of fish sauce, which can be substituted if needed. It is a salty, brown liquid extract of fish or shrimp. It serves as a background and highlights other flavors. Most oriental groceries carry fish sauce. You can substitute anchovy paste or soy sauce.

Nevertheless, Thai dishes that call for it would not be authentic without nampla. To store, seal tightly and refrigerate.

Noodles (Guay Tiew)—When a Thai asks for guey tiew, he means rice noodles in general. Rice noodles come in several sizes (big, medium, small, tiny, and vermicelli-like, (called sên mèe). Ba mèe refers to egg noodles, which are medium yellow in color. Soy bean flour (transparent) noodles are called woon sên. Noodles can be found fresh or dried. Normally, dried noodles need to be softened by soaking in cold water for about 10 minutes, then drained before cooking or following your recipe. The smaller types, like woon sên or sên mèe, require less time. If you are pressed for time, just put them in a sieve and dip into boiling water for a couple of seconds. Dried or even fresh Asian-style noodles of all kinds can be obtained in most oriental markets.

Glossary

Preserved Parsnips, Radish, Turnip or Mustard Greens—These come in vacuum-sealed jars or packages (whole or sliced), and found in oriental stores. They are used to add flavor to food as called for.

Rhizome (Zerumbet)—Krachai (in Thai), is a plant with scaly leaves—a creeping stem lying horizontally under surface of the soil, bearing leaves or aerial shoots near its tips (roots are produced from its under surface). Krachai is of the ginger family. The flavor is preferably used in Thai seafood and curry pastes. Fresh or dried rhizome can be found in Asian stores.

Rice Vinegar—Rice vinegar is preferable for Asian cooking. White rice vinegar is used for cooking and red is used for salad or added to condiments. Most Asian stores and many supermarkets carry both kinds.

Rice, Flour & Sizzling Rice Sheets—The Thai word kâo (rice), also means food, since Thai people eat rice with just about every dish. For this reason, we prefer plain and unsalted cooked rice.

As rice serves as a background, and also to tone down spicy dishes, it should be bland, white, not brown, nor converted, nor parboiled. It should always have a clean taste and be shiny looking. There are several varieties of rice: long, medium, short grain, sticky (or glutinous) sweet, new, aged, and fragrant. Thailand is well-known for its special fragrant rice called Jasmine.

Thais cook rice by an absorption method, bringing rice to a boil first, then covering and reducing heat and letting simmer until the water is absorbed. To cook good—and good-looking—rice, one has to wash it 1-2 times before cooking. An electric rice cooker is the easiest way to cook good rice. After cleaning the rice, measure about 3 cups of water for 3 cups of rice (aged rice needs about 1/2 cup more water). After the light goes off, wait for about 10 minutes before

Glossary

serving. You can also steam rice by using the same method and the same measurements, just wait until the water in the steamer boils before putting the rice in a bowl with water and cover. Rice will be cooked within 30-35 minutes. Let stand for about 10 minutes more, with the cover on, after you turn off the heat.

The best way to cook sticky, or glutinous rice, is to soak in very warm water for 20-25 minutes (cold water for 3-8 hours), drain, line the steamer with a double thickness of muslin, then put rice in the steamer (there is no need to put water in the rice). Steam about 30 minutes on medium heat. All varieties of rice, including rice flour and sizzling rice sheets (used for deep frying as appetizer with dip) can be found in most oriental stores.

Sesame Seed—White sesame seeds are used roasted in Thai desserts. For best results, before roasting, wash and dry, then fry in a dry pan on medium to low heat. Roasted sesame seeds give a wonderful flavor to your dishes.

Shrimp Paste (Kapi)—Kapi is the Thai name for dried shrimp paste, an essential ingredient in Thai cuisine. It is a brownish, concentrated paste made of fermented prawns. Even though it has a powerful aroma, once added (in small quantities) to food, the outcome is magical. For best results, roast before adding to the food by wrapping in foil and heating over a charcoal fire or in the oven. Most oriental groceries carry shrimp paste (several varieties). It should be stored tightly closed and refrigerated.

Sriracha Sauce (Thai Chili Sauce)—A Thai all-purpose sauce, cooked from chilies, vinegar, sugar, garlic, and salt. It comes in three degrees of hotness: mild, medium hot and very hot. Sriracha sauce can be found in most Asian groceries and in some supermarkets.

Tamarind & Tamarind Liquid—Tamarind, the fruit of a beautiful tropical tree, is shaped like a big bean. When it is young, the meat inside tastes sour, but when mature and has

Glossary

a brown brittle pod, the meat that covers the shiny dark seeds has a tartly sweet taste. The tart fruit paste extracted from these brown dried pods comes in packages and is sold in oriental food stores. To make the tamarind liquid that is called for in many recipes, you have to soak a piece of this brown pulp (1" x 1" in size) in about 3/4 cup of hot water for 15 minutes, squeeze to mix well, and strain through a sieve, and use the liquid accordingly.

Taro Root—The root of a large, tropical Asiatic plant of the arum family. With shield-shaped leaves, its edible corns are used to cook meals or desserts. Taro can be found fresh, frozen, or in dried chips in many oriental food stores.

Tofu (Soybean Curd or Soybean Paste)—Tofu—taohu in Thai—originated in China. It is made from cooked, fermented soybeans with malt and a little salt. Thais use this as a substitute for meat in vegetarian dishes. It can also be a substitute for cream, sour cream, or cream cheese (for cake, ice cream, dips or dressing). There are two types of tofu. The creamy and soft kind (or miso in Japanese) comes in red, brownish, and beige colors and is used in soups or sauces. The firm Chinese type of tofu comes in a cake about 1" x 3". It can be crispy fried, steamed, or boiled. Tofu is now used in Western foods, since it is full of protein and low in cholesterol and salt. With its bland taste, it picks up all flavors when added to a dish.

Turmeric (Longa, Curcuma)—This is another member of the ginger family. There are two kinds of turmeric, one with orange, carrot-like flesh, and one with white flesh. Thais use fresh, minced, or pounded to mix with other ingredients for curry paste, or just to eat fresh (white kind), with other condiments. It adds a special aromatic, pungent flavor to the food and colors any sauce yellow. Turmeric (fresh or ground) is easily found in most Asian markets.

Glossary

Wood Fungus (Cloud Ear Fungus, Jelly Mushroom)—
The Thai name is hed hunu. When dried, it has a black or grayish-black color and needs to be soaked in water before using. After about 10-15 minutes in water, it will become soft and swell up to look like a curved ear (its original state). Thais use stir-fried dishes or to add to soup. Many Thai and oriental grocery stores carry dried "hed hunu" in packets.

Thai/Asian Groceries

Thai/Asian Groceries

Alabama (AL)

Asian Food Market
417 Valley Ave
Birmingham, AL 35209
Tel (205) 941-1009

Chai's Oriental Food Store
2133 7th Ave South
Birmingham, AL 35233
Tel (205) 324-4873

Asian Supermarket
1407-A Montgomery S W
Birmingham, AL 35216
Tel (205) 822-0140

Alaska (AK)

Asian Grocery
4346 Spenard Rd
Anchorage, AK 99517
Tel (907) 248-7538

Nam San Oriental Grocery
915 West Northern Lights Blvd
Anchorage, AK 99503
Tel (907) 274-5788

Arizona (AZ)

Kim's Oriental Grocery
2205 South Cray Croft Rd
Tucson, AZ 85711
Tel (602) 790-6945

Thai/Asian Groceries

Thai Market
8816 North 43rd Ave
Glendale, AZ 85302
Tel (602) 931-8139

Thai-Laos Market
11055 North 19 Ave
Phoenix, AZ 85029
Tel (602) 678-1156

Thai Market
4130 North 83rd Ave
Phoenix, AZ 85033
Tel (602) 849-0334

Dang's Thai Market Inc
524 West Broadway Rd
Tempe, AZ 85282
Tel (602) 966-1490

Grace Oriental Market
1533 East Apache Blvd
Tempe, AZ 85281
Tel (602) 966-9233

Kim Bong Market
2620 West Broadway Rd
Mesa, AZ 85202
Tel (602) 968-7322

Arkansas (AR)

Litiszont Market
2702 North 50 North Albert Pike
Fort Smith, AR 72904
Tel (501) 783 6250

Pat's Oriental Market
503 1/2 Holcomb
Springdale, AR 72764
Tel (501) 751-1547

Thai/Asian Groceries

California (CA)

Bangkok Market Inc
4757 Melrose Ave
Los Angeles, CA 90029
Tel (213) 585-5385

Sanamluang Market
5176 Hollywood Blvd
Hollywood, CA 90027
Tel (213) 660-8000

Sanamluang Market
1670 Indian Hill Blvd
Pomona, CA 91767
Tel (714) 621-7666

Lao Pakse Market
1296 North Fresno Street
Fresno, CA 93703
Tel (209) 233-8999

K & D Market
830 East Belmont Ave
Fresno, CA 93701
Tel (209) 266-2380

Erawan Market
1474-78 University Ave
Berkeley, CA 94702
Tel (510) 849-9707

Bangkok Grocery
3236 Geary Blvd
San Francisco, CA 94118
Tel (415) 221-5863

SDS Oriental Market
919 11th Ave
Bakersfield, CA 93304
Tel (805) 721-8336

Viray Asian Grocery
27098 Hesperian Blvd
Heywood, CA 94545
Tel (510) 887-1325

Thai/Asian Groceries

Magat Asian Grocery & Trading
14624 East 14th
San Leandro, CA 94578
Tel (510) 895-0477

Asian Market
3056 Del Monte Blvd
Marina, CA 93933
Tel (408) 384-3000

Smart Oriental Market
8236 Coldwater Canyon
North Hollywood, CA 91605
Tel (213) 989-9417

Oriental Market
4205 South Fairview Ave
Goleta, CA 93117
Tel (805) 683-4417

Indochina Market
6831 Hollister Ave
Goleta, CA 93117
Tel (805) 968-3353

Nikka Oriental Groceries & Gifts
5721 Calle Real
Goleta, CA 93117
Tel (805) 964-7396

Indra Market
1361 East Colorado Blvd
Glendale, CA 91205
Tel (818) 243-8209

Lynwood Market
11325 Atlantic Ave
Lynwood, CA 90262
Tel (213) 635-9457 or (213) 537-1685

New Vientiane Market
1749 West La Palma Ave
Anaheim, CA 92801
Tel (714) 520-7995

Oriental Grocery
5527 Del Ammo Blvd
Lakewood, CA 90713
Tel (213) 866-1183

Thai/Asian Groceries

Thai-Lao Market
1721 West La Palma Ave
Anaheim, CA 92801
Tel (714) 535-2656

Thai Market
11550 Colima Rd
Whittier, CA 90604
Tel (213) 946-1435

Oriental Market
1443 Chester
Aurora, CO 80012
Tel (303) 366-0454

Thai Barn Store
2804 South Federal Blvd
Denver, CO 80236
Tel (303) 762-1931

Colorado (CO)

Krung Thai Imports
11700 Montview Blvd
Aurora, CO 80010
Tel (303) 343-9450

Thai Grocery
1001 South Federal Blvd
Denver, CO 80219
Tel (303) 935-3766

Connecticut (CT)

Bangkok Store
1932 Park St
Hartford, CT 06106
Tel (203) 236-7046

Thai/Asian Groceries

Florida (FL)

Oriental Food Mart
4245 North State Rd
7 Lauderdale Lakes
Ft Lauderdale, FL 33319
Tel (305) 485-9450

Thai Spice
1514 East Commercial Blvd
Oakland Park
Ft Lauderdale, FL 33334
Tel (305) 771-4535

Far East Food & Gift
4140 North State Rd
7 Lauderdale Lakes
Ft Lauderdale, FL 33334
Tel (305) 486-6373

Oriental Import Inc
6305 Grand National Dr
Orlando, FL 32819
Tel (407) 351-8404

Bangkok Market
17200 South Dixie Hwy
Miami, FL 33157
Tel (305) 253-5478

Oriental Grocery and Seafood Market
3355 Lake Worth Rd
Suite # 1
Lake Worth, FL 33461
Tel (407) 434-2173

Georgia (GA)

Oriental Food Store
3082 Deans Bridges Rd
Augusta, GA 30906
Tel (404) 758-9815

Thai/Asian Groceries

Kim's Oriental Market
2324 Lumpkin Rd
Augusta, GA 30906
Tel (404) 790-3431

Oriental Market
2306 Lumpkin Rd
Augusta, GA 30906
Tel (404) 793-4249

Asia Oriental Food Store
3801 Washington Rd
Martinez, GA 30907
Tel (404) 860-0674

Far East Co
411 Pennsylvania Ave
Savannah, GA 31404
Tel (912) 234-0400

Han Me Oriental Food & Gifts
2 East De Renne Ave
Savannah, GA 31405
Tel (912) 355-6411

Hong Tan Oriental Food
2802 Capitol St
(behind 1012 Gale Ct)
Savannah, GA 31404
Tel (912) 233-9184

Hawaii (HI)

Asia Grocery
1319 South Beretania St
Honolulu, HI 96814
Tel (808) 531-8371

Siam Panich Grocery
171 North Beretania St
Honolulu, HI 96813
Tel (808) 536-7440

Thai/Asian Groceries

Idaho (ID)

Oriental Gift & Food Imports
5827 Franklin Rd
Boise, ID 83709
Tel (208) 345-1301

Illinois (IL)

Bangkok Grocery
1021 West Lawrence
Chicago, IL 60640
Tel (312) 784-0001

Thailand Food Corp.
4821 North Broadway
Chicago, IL 60640
Tel (312) 728-1199

Thai Grocery
5014-16 North Broadway Ave
Chicago, IL 60640
Tel (312) 561-5345

Pna Oriental Store
2310 West Leland Ave
Chicago, IL 60625
Tel (312) 784-1797

Siam Food
7907 South State
Chicago, IL 60619
Tel (312) 783-4780

Am-KO Oriental Food
32 East Green St
Champaign, IL 61820
Tel (217) 398-2922

Do-Ray Oriental Grocery
1102 West Main St
Urbana, IL 61801
Tel (217) 384-1311

Thai/Asian Groceries

Chang's Oriental Mart
505 South Neil St
Champaign, IL 61820
Tel (217) 356-9288

The Far-East Oriental Grocery
105 South 5th St
Champaign, IL 61820
Tel (217) 352-7137

Indiana (IN)

A-1 Oriental Supermarket
3709 North Shadeland Ave
Indianapolis, IN 46226
Tel (317) 546-5252

Oriental Food Market
5344 West 38th
Indianapolis, IN 46254
Tel (317)291-1053

Iowa (IA)

Thai Market, Inc
411 1/2 East Grand Ave
Des Moines, IA 50309
Tel (515) 280-3999

Jung's Oriental Food Store
1140 East 9th St
Des Moines, IA 50316
Tel (515) 266-3891

Ting's Asian Market
1339 2nd Ave
Des Moines, IA 50314
Tel (515) 284-0527

International Groceries & More Inc
2211 Hickman Rd
Des Moines, IA 50310
Tel (515) 279-0425

Thai/Asian Groceries

Kansas (KS)

Lao Food Market
2441 South Hillside
Wichita, KS 67216
Tel (316) 686-4166

Oriental Food Market
1640 North Broadway
Wichita, KS 67214
Tel (316) 262-3670

Oriental Food Store
516 S E 29th
Topeka, KS 66605
Tel (913) 235-8354

Shin Asian Supermarket
2449 Iowa
Lawrence, KS 66061
Tel (913) 841-0140

Kentucky (KY)

Asia Grocery
2350 Woodhill Dr
Lexington, KY 40509
Tel (606) 269-7722

Louisiana (LA)

Oriental Supermarket
3562 Carrollton Ave
New Orleans, LA 70118
Tel (504) 488-1300

Thai/Asian Groceries

Maine (ME)

Asian Food Market
945 Congress
Portland, ME 04102
Tel (207) 772-3585

Maryland (MD)

Thai Market Inc
902 Thayer Ave
Silver Spring, MD 20910
Tel (301) 495-2779

International Food Market
6844 New Hampshire Ave
Takoma Park, MD 20912
Tel (301) 270-4470

Michigan (MI)

Oriental Food
20 North Heron
Ypsilanti, MI 48197
Tel (313) 487-9898

Manna International Foods & Gifts
1156 Broadway
Ann Arbor, MI 48105
Tel (313) 663-6868

Oriental Mart
2761 East Grand River
East Lansing, MI 48823
Tel (517) 337-2519

Saigon Market
655 28th St S E
Grand Rapid, MI 49548
Tel (616) 245-5851

Thai/Asian Groceries

Minnesota (MN)

Thai Hoc Grocery
818 East Lake St
Minneapolis, MN 55407
Tel (612) 824-2226

Southeast Asia Market
1001 Franklin Ave E
Minneapolis, MN 55404
Tel (612) 870-8398

M F Oriental Food Inc
747 Franklin Ave East
Minneapolis, MN 55404
Tel (612) 870-1002

King's Oriental Groceries
425 Cedar Ave South
Minneapolis, MN 55454
Tel (612) 340-0177

Lansang Grocery
1725 East Lake St
Minneapolis, MN 55407
Tel (612) 721-4883

Lao Market
2750 Nicollet Ave
Minneapolis, MN 55408
Tel (612) 874-6477

Asian Market
928 West Broadway
Minneapolis, MN 55411
Tel (612) 521-0914

Mississippi (MS)

Oriental Mart
102 Wilmington
Jackson, MS 39204
Tel (601) 372-2285

Thai/Asian Groceries

Missouri (MO)

Far Eastern Oriental Foods
7811 Wonall
Kansas City, MO 64114
Tel (816) 361-7743

Jay Asia Food
3172 South Grand St
St Louis, MO 63118
Tel (314) 772-2552

Lao Market
514 Kansas Ave
Kansas City, MO 64127
Tel (816) 281-2877

Montana (MT)

Thai's Convenience
181 Lower River Rd
Great Falls, MT 59405
Tel (406) 452-0672

Nebraska (NE)

International Spices Ltd
322 South Main St N E
Elkhorn, NE 68022
Tel (800) 362-1003

Omaha Oriental Food
2763 Farnam
Omaha, NE 68131
Tel (402) 345-1736

Thai/Asian Groceries

Aki Oriental Foods & Gifts
4425 South 84th
Omaha, NE 68127
Tel (402) 339-2671

Jung's Oriental Food Store
Suite-105 A
3031 O St
Lincoln, NE 68510
Tel (402) 435-7272

Oriental Market
612 North 27th
Lincoln, NE 68503
Tel (402) 475-0556

Nevada (NV)

International Market
95 East Grove
Reno, NV 89502
Tel (702) 825-5258

Comedy Oriental Grocery Store
2124 Greenbrae Dr
Sparks, NV 89431
Tel (702) 356-8504

Oriental Groceries & Gifts
3344 Kietzke Lane
Reno, NV 89502
Tel (702) 825-1533

International Thai Market
1802 South Main
Las Vegas, NV 89104
Tel (702) 386-9050

Thai market
3297 North Las Vegas Blvd
Las Vegas, NV 89115
Tel (702) 643-8080

Oriental Food of Las Vegas
953 East Sahara Ave
Las Vegas, NV 89104
Tel (702) 735-2788

Thai/Asian Groceries

Jimmy's Oriental Market
2017 East Charleston Blvd
Las Vegas, NV 89104
Tel (702) 355-1191

New Hampshire (NH)

Oriental Market
123 Hanover
Manchester, NH 03101
Tel (603) 668-3362

New Jersey (NJ)

Oriental Market
440 Rochelle Ave
Rochelle Park, NJ 07662
Tel (201) 843-4952

Thai's Deli
481 Washington Ave
Newark, NJ 07102
Tel (201) 759-5565

Oriental Market
845 New Rd
Pleasantville, NJ 08232
Tel (609) 383-8388

Rice Bowl Oriental Groceries
1636 Kings High Way
North Cherry Hill, NJ 08034
Tel (609) 429-1887

New Mexico (NM)

A-1 Oriental Market
2740 Wyoming Blvd N E
Albuquerque, NM 87111
Tel (505) 275-9021

Thai/Asian Groceries

Far East Oriental Market
1016 Juan Taboo Blvd N E
Albuquerque, NM 87112
Tel (505) 293-7701

Oriental Food Mart
187-16 Hillside Ave
Jamaica, NY 11432
Tel (212) 217-0120

New York (NY)

Siam Grocery
2745 Broadway
New York, NY 10025
Tel (212) 864-3640

Bangkok Village Grocery Inc
206 Thompson
New York, NY 10012
Tel (212) 777-9272

Royal Oriental Food
142-38 Roosevelt Ave
Flushing, NY 11367
Tel (212) 762-4924

North Carolina (NC)

Oriental Dong-Huong-Vietnam
1407 East Blvd
Charlotte, NC 28203
Tel (704) 568-8709

Kim Oriental Foods & Gifts*
301 Merrimon Ave
Ashville, NC 28801
Tel (704) 252-7235

Silver Wok Food & Gift Shop
US 15-501 HWY Bypass
Chapel Hill, NC 27514
Tel (919) 933-1295

Thai/Asian Groceries

Ohio (OH)

Thai Am Market
3950 Edwards Rd
Cincinnati, OH 45209
Tel (513) 631-6242

Souksavanh Grocery Store
6108 Lorain Ave
Cleveland, OH 44102
Tel (216) 651-2080

Philippines & Oriental Food Mart
4615 Pearl Rd
Cleveland, OH 44109
Tel (216) 351-0775

Thai Grocery & Gift Shop
108 East Main St
Columbus, OH 43215
Tel (614) 228-2102

Four Seas Emporium
3070 North High St
Columbus, OH 43202
Tel (614) 261-0154

International Food Co
2407 North High St
Columbus, OH 43202
Tel (614) 268-6688

Asian Grocery & Jewelry
1481 West Broad St
Columbus, OH 43222
Tel (614) 272-5981

Oklahoma (OK)

International Foods
3607 North Portland
Oklahoma City, OK 73112
Tel (405) 943-1076

Thai/Asian Groceries

Oriental Food Market
2213 South Air Depot Blvd
Oklahoma City, OK 73110
Tel (405) 732-1506

Nam-Hai Oriental Food Market
1924 Garnett Rd
Tulsa, OK 74128
Tel (918) 438-0166

Tai-Tran Asian Food Market
7727 East 21st
Tulsa, OK 74129
Tel (918) 665-7476

Oregon (OR)

Mekong Oriental Food & Gifts
1805 N E 39th
Portland, OR 97212
Tel (503) 281-7108

An-Dong Oriental Food Co
5441 S E Powell Blvd
Portland, OR 97206
Tel (503) 777-2463

Asian Market-Beaverton
12350 S W Broadway
Beaverton, OR 97201
Tel (503) 646-8118

Phong Phu Market
902 North Killingsworth
Portland, OR 97217
Tel (503) 283-3957

Rice N Spice Oriental Market
144 West 10th
Eugene, OR 97401
Tel (503) 687-9710

Sunrise Oriental Market
2160 West 11th #A
Eugene, OR 97402
Tel (503) 343-3295

Thai/Asian Groceries

A-Dong Market
2990 Silverton Rd N E
Salem, OR 97303
Tel (503) 371-3076

Pan Asia Foods
247 Atwood
Pittsburgh, PA 15213
Tel (412) 687-3236

Pennsylvania (PA)

Rhode Island (RI)

International Food Market
1916 Welsh Rd
Philadelphia, PA 19115
Tel (215) 969-1610

Oriental Mart
1900 South 15
Philadelphia, PA 19145
Tel (215) 271-9700

East Oriental Food Store
4027 Wm Penn Hwy
Monroeville, PA 15146
Tel (412) 372-1173

Asian City Market
Ocean State Job Lot Piz
Providence, RI 02904
Tel (401) 461-825

East Sea Oriental Market
90 Warren Ave East
Providence, RI 02911
Tel (401) 434-3251

T O Oriental Food Store
524 Smith
Providence, RI 02908
Tel (401) 454-5270

Thai/Asian Groceries

Tropical Market
1191 Westminster
Providence, RI 02909
Tel (401) 351-2230

South Carolina (SC)

Lynn's Imports
1266 Redbank Rd
Goose Creek
Charleston, SC 29445
Tel (803) 572-3089

Tennessee (TN)

Asian Foods
5916 Charlotte Pike
Nashville, TN 37221
Tel (615) 356-5682

Oriental Best Food Store
3710 South Mendenhall Rd
Memphis, TN 38115
Tel (901) 366-1570

Asian Grocery
4509 1/2 Summer Ave
Memphis, TN 38122
Tel (901) 683-8534

Sam's Oriental Grocery
758 Mt Moriah Rd
Memphis, TN 38117
Tel (901) 682-3569

Texas (TX)

Siam Loaf market
6929 Long Point
Houston, TX 77055
Tel (713) 618-0751

Thai/Asian Groceries

Saigon Supermarket
8282 Bellaire Blvd
Houston, TX 77036
Tel (713) 981-7038

Oriental Market
500 Pampa Dr
Austin, TX 78752
Tel (512) 454-8486

Hong Oriental Grocery & Gift Shop
2000 North Lee Trevino Dr
El Paso, TX 79936
Tel (915) 594-1858

Siam Groceries
2636 North Fitzhugh
Dallas, TX 75204
Tel (214) 823-8676

Thai Binh Oriental Market
5417 Lancaster Ave South
Dallas, TX 75241
Tel Toll Free (817) 429-2777

Thailand Market
2216 West GrauwylerRd
Dallas, TX 75221
Tel (214) 986-5855

Laos Mái Market
2441 West Walnut
Dallas, TX 75243
Tel (214) 487-6456

Lâo Store
4536 Bryan St
Dallas, TX 75204
Tel (214) 821-2878

Oriental Market Food Gift
Carrollton Park Shopping Center
Carrollton, TX 75006
Tel (214) 416-6828

Thai/Asian Groceries

Utah (UT)

Indochina Market
1616 West 3500 South
West Valley City, UT 84101
Tel (801) 975-7805

Phnom Penh Oriental Market
3582 South Redwood Rd
West Valley City, UT 84101
Tel (801) 977-0204

Oriental Food Market
667 South 700 East
Salt Lake City, UT 84102
Tel (801) 363-2122

Dong Ba Oriental Food Market
7046 South State Midvale
Salt Lake City, UT 84101
Tel (801) 561-1550

Asian Food City
758 South 200 West
Salt Lake City, UT 84101
Tel (801) 532-7426

Virginia (VA)

Oriental Market
431 East Belt Blvd
Richmond, VA 23224
Tel (804) 231-7624

Mekong Center
3107 Wilson Blvd
Arlington, VA 22201
Tel (703) 527-2779

Oriental Supermarket Inc
5001 Columbia Pike
Arlington, VA 22204
Tel (703) 671-7091

Thai/Asian Groceries

Apsara Gourmet Oriental Food Market
404 Elden St
Herndon, VA 22070
Tel (713) 471-9194

Oriental Food
4316 Markham St
Annandale, VA 22003
Tel (713) 941-8924

Asian Market
9615 15th St S W
Seattle, WA 98106
Tel (206) 762-8658

Asian Connection
409 Maynard South
Seattle, WA 98104
Tel (206) 587-6010
Fax Line (202) 343-7763

Washington (WA)

Thai Grocery
10046 15th S W
Seattle, WA 98146
Tel (206) 762-8423

Cambodian Market
9419 16th S W
Seattle, WA 98106
Tel (206) 767-0531

Wisconsin (WI)

Yue Wah Oriental Foods
2328 South Park
Madison, WI 53713
Tel (608) 257-9338

Oriental Food Mart
1212 South Park
Madison, WI 53715
Tel (608) 255-0326

Thai/Asian Groceries

Vientiane Market
1220 South 16 St
Milwaukee, WI 53204
Tel (414) 647-0019

Peace Oriental Foods & Gifts
4250 West Fond du Lac Ave
Milwaukee, WI 53216
Tel (414) 871-1818

Washington DC

China Town Market
521 H St N W
Washington, DC 20001
Tel (202) 842-0130

Mikado Grocer
Oriental Specialties
4709 Wisconsin Ave N W
Washington, D C 20016
Tel (202) 362-7700

Da Hua Market
623 H St N W
Washington, DC 20001
Tel (202) 371-8888

Wyoming (WY)

International Groceries
1609 West Lincoln Way
Cheyenne, WY 82001
Tel (307) 634-4888

185

Index

Index

Index

Index

C

Index

Index

E

Index

Index

G

Index

H

I

Index

Index

Index

Index

O

P

Index

Index

Index

Index

Index

Index

Index

Index

Y

Z

10/93

mLib